OLD JOLIET PRISON

OLD JOLIET PRISON

WHEN CONVICTS WORE STRIPES

AMY KINZER STEIDINGER

THE History PRESS

Published by The History Press
Charleston, SC
www.historypress.com

Front cover, clockwise from top left: courtesy Will County Historical Museum and Research Center; courtesy Joliet Area Historical Museum; courtesy Will County Historical Museum and Research Center; courtesy Joliet Area Historical Museum; courtesy Joliet Area Historical Museum.
Back cover, left inset: courtesy of *Chicago Tribune*; *right inset*: courtesy Joliet Area Historical Museum.

First published 2020

Manufactured in the United States

ISBN 9781467147361

Library of Congress Control Number: 2020941938

Notice: The information in this book is true and complete to the best of our knowledge. It is offered without guarantee on the part of the author or The History Press. The author and The History Press disclaim all liability in connection with the use of this book.

To my very supportive and encouraging husband, Jay; my brother and favorite photographer, Adam; my mom, Denise, who has always been my greatest cheerleader; and my kids, who have grown up to be amazing adults.

CONTENTS

PREFACE

My first book, *So Many Fragile Things*, told the story of Samuel Moser, who was sentenced to the Illinois State Penitentiary at Joliet in 1901. He died there in 1910, shortly before he was to be released. I had done some research and become fascinated with the history of the old prison on Collins Street. In the fall of 2019, my brother and I heard that the prison was being opened for tours. We ordered tickets and planned a day trip.

We stood in the parking lot with the other tourists who were arriving and gazed up at the imposing walls. Pictures don't prepare you. I imagined Sam being brought here, facing years inside those limestone walls. Then I thought about how many thousands of other stories this building represented. The historian in me was imagining the time periods—the Civil War, the turn of the century, Prohibition, the Depression, the World Wars, Vietnam. Then, a look-alike of the Blues Brothers' mobile pulled up (with the loudspeaker strapped to the roof, even!), and I was completely hooked—I just wanted to hear every single story.

ACKNOWLEDGEMENTS

Thanks to the reporters who originally told these stories and took us along on their visits to the prison.

Thanks to Heather Bigeck and the Joliet Area Historical Museum for help and encouragement in the completion of this project. For more information, visit jolietmuseum.org.

Thanks to Sandy Vasko and the Will County Historical Society and Research Center just a few short miles north in Lockport, Illinois. For more information, visit willhistory.org.

Thanks to Ben Gibson at The History Press, who was such an encouragement through the many steps of the process.

Thanks to the many historical and genealogical society volunteers everywhere, who lovingly tend to the records.

INTRODUCTION

The stories in *Old Joliet Prison: When Convicts Wore Stripes* are taken directly from online newspaper archives unless otherwise noted. Though they have been blended, abbreviated, reworded for clarity and greatly simplified, efforts have been made to retain the language of the day. The result are very brief mentions of complicated true-crime stories. My intention is to give the reader what I wished for on the prison tour: a quick glimpse of many different people who lived and worked in the old prison. The reader is encouraged to further research stories of interest; many of them could be a book by themselves!

The *Cincinnati Enquirer* of March 18, 1883, had the following report:

> *The majority of desperate criminals who have become known to the Eastern police move West, land in Chicago, and then perhaps take up their temporary or permanent residence in Joliet, behind the massive prison bars. The penitentiary here is conducted on modern and humane principles, which make the incarceration of the convict as pleasant as possible consistent with proper punishment and rigid discipline.*
>
> *But life in the big pen is not a bed of roses, as all who have experienced it can abundantly testify. The murderer or burglar is kept constantly at work during the day, with only a short recess for meals, and when night comes on, he is locked in his cell, to remain until daylight brings with it the same monotonous drudgery and surveillance.*

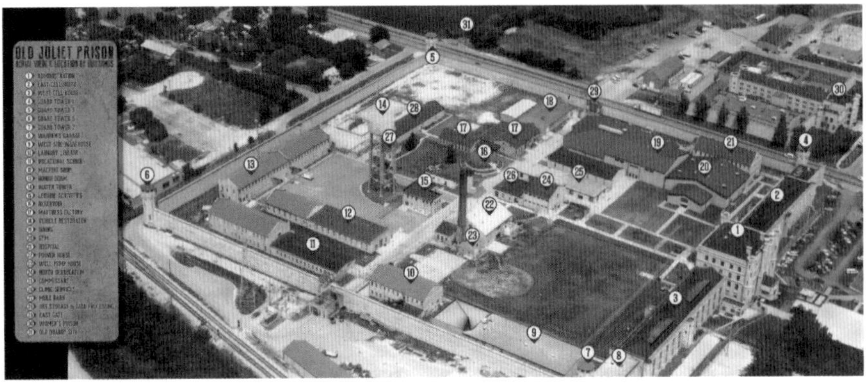

Above: An aerial view with the locations of the buildings. *Courtesy Joliet Area Historical Museum, Illinois.*

Left: A look over the massive stone walls of the administration building. *Courtesy Joliet Area Historical Museum, Illinois.*

With 1,400 of the most daring thieves and cut-throats that ever cursed a civilized country under their charge, it is not presumed that the prison officials should exhibit much tenderness and impress the condemned that they are guests of the State instead of a lot of outlaws, who must be caged and watched like so many wild animals. Once in a while there is a prisoner who deserves pity and compassion, but the majority of the Joliet gang are old-timers, who are vicious rather than unfortunate.

Of course, they are all innocent, for it has become an aphorism, from the observation of nearly all prison officials, that the bigger the thief the more virtuous indignation he exhibits at being called one. If doing a third term in the penitentiary, he is a much-persecuted individual, and is serving in martyrdom the sentence of another man who did the job. Hundreds of criminals work themselves into the belief that they are targets for the law and police when any crime is committed in the locality where they may happen to be.

1

JOLIET PRISON IN THE NEWS, *1850–80*

The Illinois State Penitentiary at Joliet

In 1847, when prison activist Dorothea Dix was asked to visit the prison at Alton, Illinois, she found the prisoners shackled with eight-foot-long chains from their waists to their ankles. They worked from dawn to dark and slept on beds made of straw. They even ate standing up. Two men lived in damp, unheated stone cubicles, and there were no bath facilities. They were made to be completely silent at all times. Punishment for violation of the rules ranged from five to forty-five lashes. There was no thought to moral guidance or reform. Dorothea pushed hard to close the Alton prison, using her platform to make the public aware of the inhumane living conditions of men who needed a chance to change their lives for the better.

With the population of Illinois quickly expanding, a new prison was needed. The crime rate was increasing rapidly, and it was expensive to transport prisoners downstate to the outdated prison at Alton. The suggested location of Joliet offered huge amounts of limestone in the ground—inmates wouldn't be able to tunnel their way out, and the limestone could be quarried on-site to build the prison walls.

Seventy-two acres were purchased along Collins Street, two miles north of the city, for about $100 an acre. Ground was broken in the late summer of 1857. The Chicago firm of Boyington and Wheelock was commissioned for the job. William W. Boyington would later design the Illinois State Capitol in Springfield and the Chicago Water Tower, famous for surviving the Great

Chicago Fire of 1871. The plan was for a fifteen-acre spot enclosed by walls five feet thick at the bottom, two feet thick at the top and twenty-five feet high, with a series of guard towers.

The structure itself was castle-like, its massive limestone walls as much as forty feet high. It reflected a time when prisoners were treated very differently than they are today. There would be a staggering 1,100 cells, with 100 for solitary confinement and 100 for women, with two wings of cells on each side of the warden's quarters. In December 1857, the *Joliet Signal* reported:

> *The penitentiary when completed, according to the plan of the commissioners, will not be excelled by an institution of the kind in the United States. It will be capable of holding one thousand convicts. The outer wall will enclose a square of eight hundred feet or about fifteen acres. The main buildings and style of the architecture, as appears from the specifications, will surpass anything yet seen in the prisons of this country.*

The first thirty-three inmates arrived from Alton to begin construction in May 1858. They lived in what was later the segregation unit. They broke chunks of limestone at a nearby quarry and built the prison that would later house them. Eventually, 160 prisoners would supply the labor force, with more inmates arriving as cells were completed. The use of convict labor kept costs low, with the total price tag for the project estimated at $75,000. It would be the largest in the country, and its design would become a model for U.S. prisons.

On May 16, 1858, three women were transferred from Alton Prison to the new penitentiary at Joliet. While the men were building the new prison, these women would cook and do the laundry. Three months later, a fire at Alton destroyed the women's unit. The women who remained there were sent to Joliet. According to the *Chicago Tribune* of February 24, 1859: "At Joliet, the new State prison is beginning to show its massive outlines, and within which the stone hammer is to be the moralizer and these blocks of magnesian lime, the subject to remind its inmates of days of innocence."

The last prisoners were transferred in July 1860. When the Civil War broke out less than a year later, eight hundred convicts were serving time in Joliet. For the next four years, both criminal prisoners and prisoners of war were kept there. The prison supported itself with convict laborers working in stone quarries, on farms and in nearby mills. But escapes from the labor force were frequent, and things became even more complicated with competition for work between the prison chain gangs and soldiers returning from the Civil War.

Joliet Prison was a primitive, difficult environment for the men who lived there. In 1877, there were reports of brutality in the disciplining of prisoners in "solitary confinement." Whipping and gagging were said to be standard punishments, and prisoners were routinely tied to the iron doors of their cells. Rather than helping, a prison physician recommended that "sound-deadened" walls be installed in the solitary quarters. It was reported that prisoners often feigned insanity, hoping to be removed from the prison.

A PRISONER WAS QUOTED in the *Chicago Tribune* of July 23, 1863:

> *Will your honor grant me more time before I am sent to Joliet? I wish to correspond with my wife and children, and if possible, see them once more before I am immured in that living tomb.*

Joliet had a reputation as one of the toughest places to do time. Two men shared a cell that was about four feet wide and seven feet high. The cell had an iron bunk bed with scratchy straw mattresses. Long before electricity, prisoners relied on natural light. Even on the brightest day, only a dull film of sun filtered into each cell. Prisoners ate and relieved themselves in cells that did not have running water or toilets. The cellmates shared a bucket for water and a bucket for human waste. Men who were doing backbreaking physical labor were allowed to bathe just once a week. Conditions were unsanitary, and the stench was overwhelming.

And yet, many news reports led people to believe that the convicts were pampered. In 1863, the *Chicago Tribune* reported: "The food is excellent, and probably better than many of the convicts were accustomed to prior to their entrée within prison walls. The bread is pure, clean and wholesome, and of a snowy whiteness which might be envied by many a housekeeper. The same excellence obtains with the meat and vegetables, and the cooking, being done by professional cooks who had the misfortune to become convicts, the prisoners thereby secure excellent meals."

Whether praising or blaming, newspaper reports out of Joliet Prison let us see what went on behind the walls of the penitentiary. Though they reflect the politics and prejudices of the times, the stories are also just human—both good and bad. As the *Chicago Inter-Ocean* newspaper once wrote, "The

penitentiary furnishes an ever-fruitful theme for newspapers because the various phases of prison life are of unceasing interest to the public."

Here are the stories, the struggles, the lives and the deaths—from "when convicts wore stripes."

Opposite: An original cell, seven feet deep by four feet wide by seven feet high. *Courtesy Joliet Area Historical Museum, Illinois.*

Above: Men on the cellblock wait to be let into their cells. *Courtesy Joliet Area Historical Museum, Illinois.*

EARLY ESCAPE ATTEMPTS

On March 1, 1859, the *Joliet Signal* reported the first escape from the new penitentiary. The convict had let himself down through a window with a rope. Before he left, he'd broken open the trunk of the "lady" of one of the prison contractors and stolen diamonds and jewelry worth $1,000.

In early November 1860, five convicts were near a gate when some visitors were passing through. Seizing the guard, they knocked him down with a hammer, wrested his musket from him and scampered away. The guard regained his feet, pursued the men and overtook them. He shot two of them in the legs with his revolver and, after a desperate scuffle, retook his musket from the third. Two other guards pursued the other escapees and captured them without resistance.

THE WAGONMAKER'S SHOP BURNED

In January 1862, the wagonmaker's shop in the penitentiary was destroyed by fire. The large stone building, together with a large quantity of wagons, harnesses and tools, was a loss of about $15,000.

ATTEMPTED MUTINY

In late August 1865, a mutinous plot was uncovered. A man named George W. Smith obtained a situation as a guard at the prison. He would be paid if he could work a plan by which several convicts could escape, When the three men succeeded in getting up on the wall, the unfaithful guard even fired on them as a cover, being careful not to hit them. Two of the convicts succeeded in making it over. Another guard, who was not in on the secret, shot at them from another portion of the wall, killing one of the convicts. The third inmate was captured and returned to his cell.

Warden Samuel Buckmaster and the deputy warden were suspicious of the undercover guard. They promoted the man to the position of night guard in the cellhouse, where he would have the opportunity to communicate freely with the prisoners. A convict was employed to gain Smith's confidence. Smith took the bait. Another guard was concealed under the detective convict's bedstead in the cell, where he laid three successive nights, overhearing everything that passed between Smith and the convict. Smith told the convict that he was engaged in maturing two plans by which to raise a general mutiny and stampede. The first was to enable the prisoners to get possession of the armory, after telling them where the key was concealed; the officers of the penitentiary would be shot, and the prisoners would be liberated.

The other plan was to secure his restoration to his former position as guard on the wall, where he always had eight or ten loaded muskets at his command. He would leave the lower door to his tower unfastened. The convicts would rush up, seize the muskets and then allow the escape of the other convicts by shooting the remainder of the guards and officers of the prison.

On the third night of hearing these plans and confessions, the concealed guard gave a signal from his hiding place under the bed. The deputy warden entered and unlocked the cell, bringing out the concealed guard. Knowing he was finished, Smith admitted the rest of the network. He was taken to the county jail.

At Work in the Quarry

In May 1866, a number of convicts at work in a stone quarry about a mile from the prison attempted to escape. When they were fired on by guards, one of the convicts was killed and another dangerously wounded; the others surrendered. A coroner's jury was summoned and rendered the verdict of justifiable homicide. The reporter for the *Joliet Signal* wrote that it was hoped that the next legislature would require the convicts to be worked within the prison walls. He argued that if this were done, authorities would not so frequently be called on to chronicle these events.

The quarry northeast of the prison across Collins Street, where men broke limestone. It was backbreaking work but a chance to get outside. *Courtesy Joliet Area Historical Museum, Illinois.*

The First Execution at Joliet Prison

George Chase was convicted as a horse thief during the Civil War. He was sent to Joliet to serve his time. The inmate struck the deputy warden with a large stone he had brought back from the quarry concealed in the sleeve of his coat. The man died a few weeks later from the injury. On July 27, 1866, Chase was the first man executed at Joliet Prison. When it was done, Chase's head was removed so that his brain could be examined by doctors. They hoped to find the cause of his criminal behavior. They announced that "the brain was sound, showing no signs of insanity." The head was given to a phrenologist for use in his lectures. The rest of George Chase was buried in the prison cemetery.

Scarcely a Week Passed

In August 1866, some twenty prisoners managed to get sledges, bars and hammers and make an assault on one of the large iron doors. They went to work battering down the door, but a few shots fired by the guards from the towers and the tops of the walls caused them to surrender. Four or five of the prisoners were severely wounded.

In December, five convicts escaped by getting into a sewer and creeping to liberty. Heavy iron bars, which protected the sewer both on the inside where they entered, and on the outside where they got out, had been sawed off and taken out by persons outside of the walls who no doubt were colluding with the convicts.

Just a few weeks later, in early January 1867, the residents of Joliet and Lockport were notified of a revolt in the penitentiary. Citizens quickly armed themselves and went to the rescue. It was true that an extensive plan had been concocted by the prisoners, but the plot had been frustrated by Buckmaster and the prison authorities.

Toward the end of January, the attempt was even more serious. A convict overpowered a guard and liberated about thirty of his fellow convicts. They extinguished the lights and set to work cutting off the large bolts that secured the doors of all the cells. Guards on the outside of the department saw that the lights were out and rushed to the rescue.

In February, there was another close call. A reporter for the *Joliet Signal* wrote:

A line of convicts marches in lockstep. *Courtesy Joliet Area Historical Museum, Illinois.*

> *It has of late become a common occurrence for convicts to escape from the penitentiary near this city. Scarcely a week passes that we do not hear of a stampede. On Wednesday last about a dozen, including the notorious burglar, Jim Wilson, escaped. Seven were recaptured, but the balance including Wilson, are yet at large. The warden and guards, it is said, are not to blame for these frequent escapes of convicts. Since the close of the war, the penitentiary has been filled by a class of prisoners that have no fear of bayonets or rifles. Indeed, many of them care no more about being shot at than they do to engage in labor. Perhaps such a hardened and experienced set of desperadoes were never collected in a prison before. At all events, the luxury of being warden or a guard is not a desirable one.*

HOMESICK AND HEARTBROKEN

In 1867, John Carney was a well-to-do pork packer in Chicago. By long years of hard work, he had acquired a competence and had reared an interesting family. Somehow, he had come into possession of a quantity of stolen goods. Carney was convicted and sentenced to three years in the penitentiary. He was placed in the prison stone quarry, where he labored for eleven months.

One day, he escaped. He took the railroad track to Lockport and from there walked to Chicago. Afraid he'd be arrested if he stayed at home, he went to St. Louis, where he remained until 1876. He missed his family and decided to give himself up. He wrote to his brother-in-law in Chicago, thinking that he might as well turn him in and collect the reward of twenty-five dollars.

Convicts Shot

In May 1867, some convicts were loading a boat on the canal opposite the prison. One of them—a stout, burly fellow—disobeyed orders. When one of the contractors reprimanded him, the convict made at him with a large stone in his fist. A guard saw the movement and fired, killing him instantly.

Less than a month later, a missing convict was spied trying to make his escape by scaling the wall. He was hailed three times but paid no attention. He was shot and so severely wounded that he survived only a few hours. The convict was serving a sentence for burglary but had only been at Joliet Prison for ten days.

A few months later, three prisoners seized a guard, disarmed him and attempted to escape. Other guards fired at them, and two were recaptured. The third ran in the direction of the canal, and his body was later found there. The injured man had drowned.

A Murder on Chicago's Lakeshore

William Gumbleton sold some property, intending to start a store in the West. He deposited his money in the bank. He and a man named Ziegenmeyer, who had come with him from Baltimore, took a walk out through Lincoln Park and along the lakeshore. Ziegenmeyer returned to the city alone and set out to impersonate Gumbleton and take his money from the bank.

Gumbleton's body was discovered in the lake a week after the crime was committed. The chief of detectives traced the murderer to Germany, where the man had used his ill-gotten wealth to buy out a starch factory in his native town. Ziegenmeyer was extradited to the United States and convicted on circumstantial evidence. Powerful friends in Germany tried for years to obtain his release from prison, without success. He served eight years of a life sentence and died of consumption in 1879, maintaining his innocence to the last.

Noted Cracksmen Escape

In 1868, Billy Dalton and George Barker, noted cracksmen, escaped from Joliet by donning suits and joining a party of visitors escorted by the warden. They passed through the yard and went out the west gate to the train. The guard on duty there did not challenge the men, because he thought they were under the charge of the warden. Barker was recaptured but escaped again in 1869 from no. 1 boiler-house, where he was employed as an engineer.

Convict No. 791

Joe Brown had quite a history in criminal and police circles in Chicago. In 1867, he nearly killed an ex-detective. He served a year for this at Joliet Prison. In 1868, Joe and noted female thief Mary Doyle burglarized a large dry-goods store. They were arrested and taken back to Joliet and sentenced to eight years each.

One day, as he was passing across the yard from his shop to another, Brown came face to face with a party of visitors. Among them was a man who once appeared as a witness in court against him. The presence of this visitor so enraged the convict that he lunged to attack the man. He was seized by an officer before any harm was done. After a week in solitary confinement, Brown was sent back to work. But one day, Joe Brown was missing from the evening count. A search failed to locate him. The man who had been threatened requested a couple of officers for protection. That night, a man was caught prowling about the house. After a desperate struggle, they succeeded in capturing convict no. 791.

Fire at the Penitentiary

In January 1868, a fire broke out in the stonecutter's shop, destroying all the wooden portions of the building. Its contents consisted of a large number of barrels, 140,000 hoop poles, 300 seasoned wagon axles, a lot of cut stone and about 500 bushels of onions. The fire originated from a defective flue. American Fire Company No. 1 and a large number of citizens had hurried to fight the fire. Because of the distance to the prison and the scarcity of water, they were unable to accomplish much. A convict named John Williams was the first to discover the fire and was instrumental in saving the stable, horses,

Construction of a new shop. Notice the men working in the top of the stack. *Courtesy Will County Historical Museum and Research Center.*

mules and other property. He'd been serving five years for larceny but was pardoned for meritorious conduct.

In February, the cooper shop also burned. The fire company was able to keep the blaze from spreading to other buildings, but the shop itself was consumed. It was noted that the prisoners had been given newspapers that told of Williams's heroics and the resulting pardon. Reporters said that this was "virtually offering a reward for incendiarism, as fires are wanted by the convicts in order to give them a chance to win pardons."

Billy Forrester

Billy Forrester was sent to Joliet in April 1868 and escaped in August. He was captured in September 1868 and escaped again two months later. One of the more successful attempts was told by Captain McDonald, deputy warden, in an interview in 1883:

> *Billy was always trying to escape and after a while succeeded. Mike Kennedy was a consumptive fellow and was given many privileges because he was thought harmless. But for this very reason he was utilized by the more desperate ones in the plot. He got hold of a suit of citizen's clothes and proceeded to the southeast tower where a new guard was on duty. He called to the guard, telling him that he had a note for him. The guard lowered his little basket by means of a rope; the note was deposited in it and it was drawn up. The note directed that the guard should report at once to the Deputy's office. Supposing Kennedy to be a guard, and not being acquainted with all the guards, he came down, unlocked the door, gave up the key and went off.*
>
> *He had no sooner got out of sight than thirteen convicts filed out of the soap yard, where they had lain concealed. Hastily entering the tower, they ascended and took charge of the dozen stand of guns always at that time kept in the towers. The convicts immediately opened fire on the guard over the gate and upon myself, and we returned the fire. The bullets fell pretty thickly around my sentry box, but neither of us were hit. Finally, the convicts ceased firing and descended on the outside. I started at once for the woods to head them off, while Warden Dornblaser and a party of guards made a hasty detour around south of them and headed them all off except Forrester.*
>
> *The warden returned with the recaptured convicts, and Forrester reached the woods. But just as he was about to climb the fence, I arose and covered*

> *him with my revolver. Billy swore he would die before he would return and started to run. I fired low, wounding him in one of the legs and dropping him. He returned then all right, but subsequently sawed out of the wing and escaped. That time he was gone for about four years.*

When financier Benjamin Nathan was murdered, detectives believed the word of a convict informant and pursued Forrester, though he had been in the South at the time. He was cleared in that case but brought back to Joliet to finish serving his time. He served thirteen years and was out again in 1880.

SPECIAL DELIVERIES

In May 1868, an express wagon came to the prison to pick up a supply of boots. The driver was informed by the foreman of the shop that there was no work ready. Having business in another part of the prison, he left his wagon for a few moments. When he returned, he found that a large box had been loaded into the wagon. Supposing it was a box of goods that the foreman had decided to send after he had spoken to him, he got into the wagon and drove off. When near the railroad crossing between the prison and the city, he heard a noise from the wagon. The lid of the box was lifted; two convicts crawled out, jumped off the wagon and ran. The driver immediately reported the escape. A pursuit ensued, and one of the escaped convicts was captured. The other was cornered in an area where a young man was practicing with a revolver. The unarmed guard requested that the youth shoot the convict. He did, wounding him in the shoulder. Both convicts were then returned to the prison.

LOOKING FOR HOMES FOR THE WINTER

It was said that the number of convicts at the prison was increasing: "All the rascals in the land seem to be looking for homes for the winter."

WHISKEY, FILTH AND IDLENESS

In September, it was noted that "six of the dirtiest looking scabs ever received in poor house or prison were brought up from Cairo—hatless and bootless,

A team of horses pull a wagon through the prison yard. Notice the guard on the tower. *Courtesy Will County Historical Museum and Research Center.*

ragged, filthy, and hungry. The General gave them the first bath they had probably had in their lives, clothed them in stripes, and set them to work. The rascals are no doubt better off than they ever were before and take their rations with a gusto and relish that whiskey, filth and idleness have deprived them of heretofore."

Raised from the Dead

In May 1869, the chaplain of the penitentiary and some convict helpers were carrying a casket to the cemetery for burial. The solemn procession was brought to a sudden halt by unearthly screams issuing from the coffin. The pious chaplain and mourners dropped the coffin as though it was a red-hot iron. The lid of the coffin was opened. Instead of the dead African American convict they'd put into the box, a live man of fair complexion sat upright. It was later discovered that the body of the dead man had been removed and hidden under a pile of stones. The other man had convinced some comrades to nail the lid over him temporarily so that he could escape from the procession once it reached the cemetery. The atmosphere of the house of the dead, however, became suffocating so that he was forced to cry for help before the procession had passed the outer wall of the prison, and his cunning plan to escape was ended. The convict was ordered to his cell, and the body of the other man was pulled out from under the stones and replaced in the coffin.

The Prison Is Completed

The cornerstone was laid in 1857, but the prison was not completed until 1869. The exterior view was imposing and picturesque. The four-story center building included the warden's house, which contained the offices, the guards' hall, commissioners' rooms, dining rooms, armory and officers' sleeping rooms. On either side of the warden's house extended the great cellhouse wings, each three hundred feet long, giving the institution a frontage toward the south of nearly one thousand feet.

According to S.W. Wetmore in his 1892 book *Behind the Walls of Joliet*:

> *The exterior of the prison impresses the visitor, and at first sight suggests one of those old castles of the olden time, those romantic structures*

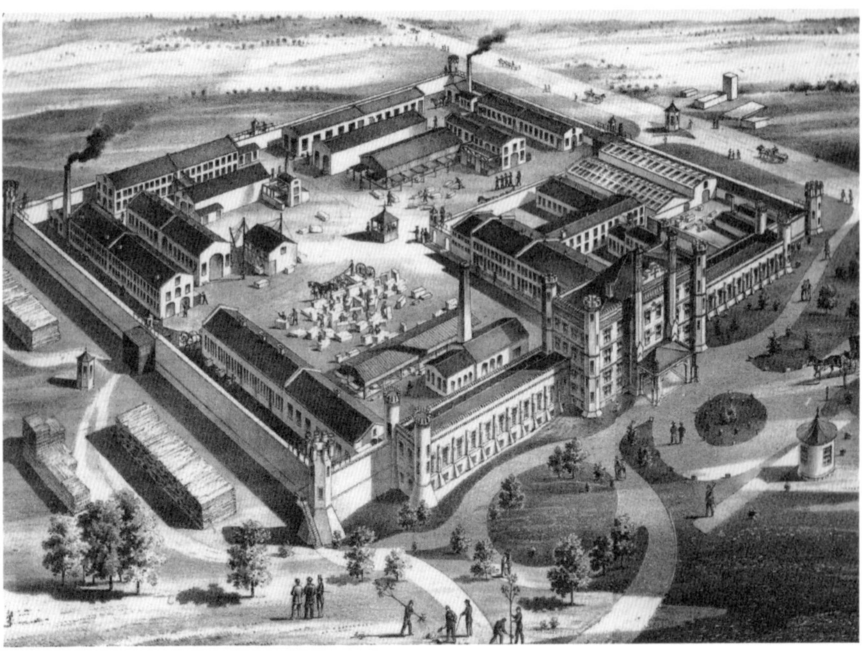

An early illustration of the Illinois State Penitentiary—a virtual city within its walls. *David Rumsey Map Collection.*

that withstood the ancient archers and warring elements for ages. The battlemented walls upon which blue-coated men with Winchester rifles under their arms patrolling platforms that surround the rugged but ornamental towers help to make up the romantic picture, which is finally dispelled when the eye rests upon the iron-barred windows, proclaiming that it is a prison.

KNIVES OUT

At the beginning of May 1869, a gang from the prison was headed to the quarries under a charge of guards. A quarrel between two convicts became a desperate fight with knives. Both combatants were wounded, one of them so severely that he died the following day.

Only a few days later, another quarrel occurred when the inmates were sitting down to dinner. A few words passed between two large and powerful men. They both drew knives, and a deadly struggle ensued. They fought the entire length of one of the long tables, stabbing and striking alternately. By the time they were separated, they had begun to fail from the loss of blood. They were taken to the hospital. One of them expired soon after, having been stabbed half a dozen times. The other was dangerously wounded but survived.

THE NEW RULE

In August 1869, John Phelps, who was a kitchen guard at the penitentiary, was sitting on a chair conversing with a convict. Another convict, whom he had reported to the warden for some violation of the prison rules, assaulted him with a heavy club. He fell to the floor, mortally wounded.

Later that month, eight convicts escaped. The lack of discipline at the prison was widely criticized. An investigation was made by the governor and a new order of discipline launched in October. It was said that the new rule was to shoot any convict who disobeyed orders.

KINDLING DELIVERY

In November 1869, a convict induced two of his fellows to secret him under shavings used for kindling and deliver him to one of the upper rooms of the building. There, he tied sheets together and lowered himself to the ground from one of the windows. A reporter quipped that "the 'kindling' reached terra firma and went on its way rejoicing."

FEMALE INMATES: A PERNICIOUS INFLUENCE

Robert E. Sterling writes in his 2003 book *Joliet Prisons: Images in Time*:

> *The men's cellhouses became overcrowded in 1870, so prison officials decided to move the two dozen female prisoners to the top floor of the administration building, just above the warden's quarters, and to use the women's cellhouse for male inmates. The decision to relocate the women was also justified on other grounds. The chaplain expressed concern about the "pernicious influence" of female inmates on the morality of male prisoners. It was not good, he said, for the male prisoners to live in such close proximity to "a large number of depraved females."*
>
> *From 1870 to 1895, female inmates remained imprisoned on the fourth floor of the administration building, far removed from male prisoners. For twenty-five years, the only day female inmates were permitted to descend the*

A rare outing for the women of Joliet Prison. *Courtesy Joliet Area Historical Museum, Illinois.*

four flights of stairs and venture outside was the Fourth of July. Finally, in 1895, the warden relaxed the policy and began allowing the women to go outside for Sunday afternoon walks.

The Big Break

The most desperate and determined attempt to beat the Joliet Prison was the revolt led by Luke Smith, a burglar from Chicago doing a ten-year sentence. On May 18, 1870, nearly three hundred men were engaged in this big break on the east gate.

Years later, in 1883, Captain McDonald who was by then deputy warden, talked about this break in an interview:

I shall never forget—I was then outside guard at the west gate, and had in the sentry box several double barreled shot guns, a couple of muskets, and a brace of Colt's revolvers, besides a small Smith & Wesson pocket pistol—a regular arsenal—but the whole outfit was not worth one of the sixteen shooting rifles we now use. A well-conceived plot for a general charge upon this gate to liberate the entire prison was planned among the most desperate convicts then confined here, and the sequel shows how desperately successful for a time it proved.

On the appointed day twenty-five of those plotters suddenly left their places and deliberately proceeding to a place where they had concealed guns, armed themselves and arched for the gate where I was stationed. The guns seemed to be new muskets, and each man carried besides this what appeared to be a large sized navy revolver and a knife. They came up to the gate led by the desperate and notorious Luke Smith, a twenty-five-year burglar and robber of the worst type. Billy Forester also assisted in leading the gang which gradually increased to two or three hundred, but by the time they reached the gate the number reduced to the original twenty-five, the rest losing courage and going back to work. Smith called to the guard on the wall after ordering the convicts to present their guns at him, to throw down his arms and then lie down on the wall upon his stomach. The guard obeyed, and the convicts ordered the gate opened which was done.

The battle—I commenced firing carefully at this juncture, every shot bringing down a man, and before they had got outside a dozen of them lay stretched upon the ground about the gate. I wondered why they did not

> *fire. Smith, in terrible desperation rushed up to the window of my sentry box and presenting a revolver ordered me to surrender, I replied with a shot from one of my pistols and Smith fell. I had discovered that the guns and revolvers with which they were armed were only imitation of guns made of gas pipe and well-turned stocks but they were the most perfect false arms I ever saw. The guards from both towers were playing on them and I stepped outside and continued firing till all but three had been shot down and they were captured by a detachment of guards sent out to head them off. Smith had been only stunned when he fell and was gone when the firing ceased. He ran out to the woods and just as he thought he was free a guard jumped out from behind a tree and ordered him to halt. He drew a knife and made a lunge at the guard, but a well-directed shot was sent whizzing through his brain killing him instantly. This ended the struggle.*

The wounded were carried to the hospital on stretchers. When the excitement was over, a count was made. One convict, a seven-year man named James Ferguson, was missing. He was never recaptured. The guards were commended for excellent service.

ILLINOIS STATE REFORM SCHOOL AT PONTIAC

On June 23, 1871, the Illinois State Reform School at Pontiac was opened. It was a facility for male first-time offenders, aged sixteen to twenty-six. The Illinois Teachers Association had secured the enactment of a law to create the facility in 1867. Social reformers objected to young men being placed with dangerous adult felons. (Joliet had several boys "of tender age," one little fellow being only eleven years old). It was hoped that young offenders would have a better chance for reform in an environment dedicated to educating and training young men to lead productive lives. While it was certainly a huge improvement, it didn't work for everyone. Many of the news articles from the years after it opened described inmates of Joliet as formerly incarcerated at the Pontiac reformatory.

THE GREAT CHICAGO FIRE

Nearly one thousand freshly baked loaves of bread of the finest quality were made every day in the prison bakery. Convict workers kneaded dough, put

Workers march by the chair shop. *Courtesy Will County Historical Museum and Research Center.*

the unbaked loaves into pans and arranged them in rows along the stone floor, ready for the ovens. Two huge rotary ovens were in use, the floors of which were revolved by steam power. Ten barrels of flour were baked into three-foot loaves each day. In the slicing room were several carloads of mammoth loaves ready for the next day's meals. From October 8 through 10, 1871, the Great Chicago Fire burned, killing approximately 300 people, destroying roughly 3.3 square miles of Chicago and leaving more than 100,000 residents homeless. While destitute people were homeless and starving for food, the prisoners at Joliet kept the ovens booming and red-hot all the time, baking vast quantities of bread, which they forwarded to the Relief Committee in Chicago for the suffering thousands. A great many inmates in the prison were from Chicago, and news of the fire weighed heavily on everyone.

A Close Call

In April 1873, the guard who had charge of the boot and shoe shop was attacked by a convict. He would have been killed had another convict not come to his assistance. As soon as the guard gained his feet, he drew his revolver to shoot the inmate, but the convicts took it away from him. Peace was restored, but there were 75 guards at the prison and 1,400 convicts. The people of Joliet were understandably nervous, as stories like this were becoming the norm.

A Cold-water Bath

A convict reported having sore hands and didn't perform his assigned amount of work. The prison physician ordered a cold-water bath as punishment. The inmate died as he was being taken out of the water. The postmortem examination showed a rupture of the walls of the heart. An editorial in the *Joliet Signal* said: "The unfortunate man was evidently a victim of the cruelty and ignorance of prison officials; and the taking of his life in the manner detailed comes little short of murder in the first degree. The poor convict for a trivial offence was dragged to the fatal tub and literally drowned. The matter should undergo a thorough investigation."

Major Robert Wilson McClaughry

Major Robert W. McClaughry was made warden of the penitentiary on August 1, 1874. An advocate of the new penology that favored remedial instead of purely retributive treatment, he argued that by turning a deaf ear to a convict's desire to reform and make an honest living, society could drive him back to a criminal career. He proposed the establishment of a state bureau to assist these men in securing employment.

McClaughry also believed in discipline within the prison. The consequence of more or less time or the ration of four ounces of tobacco, the privilege of writing to friends once in five weeks, the privilege of receiving weekly papers from the outside and of making overtime money were used to penalize or reward inmates. More severe infractions were met with solitary confinement. The "ducking (or drowning) the ringbolt," and other forms of cruelty were abolished.

The *Wilmington Advocate* agreed with McClaughry: "Society has moral duties to the imprisoned. A jail should be also an educator. We conceive that to be the most perfect prison system which carries these two ideas together, and in their proper relation to each other and the welfare of society; a place of punishment, but not of torture: Where mercy mitigates penalty, and love stimulates hopes of a better future." Thus the preaching and teaching of

The library was considered the first line of reform. *Courtesy Joliet Area Historical Museum, Illinois.*

the chaplain, the library of five thousand volumes of good books and a wholesome diet were means to stimulate positive change.

A Chicago publisher pronounced the prison library the best-selected library in the state. Most public libraries were filled up with twenty or more copies of the same work by the same author to accommodate the public. They were unable to keep a very large list of authors. The prison library had not two books alike from one author—only one of a kind by any one author—and thus was able to keep in supply works of all authors of any note. There was a healthy budget to purchase more books monthly and issue a regularly published catalog of what was available.

Citizens were asked and encouraged to donate books for the greater purpose of educating and reforming the unfortunate men, who needed to keep their minds busy while incarcerated.

New reading rooms were fitted up by the warden for the use of the guards, as well. They were comfortably arranged, heated by steam and lit with gas.

OSCAR SNOW

In 1874, eighteen-year-old Oscar Snow of Kiamishe, Choctaw Nation, was charged with conspiring to murder a woman's husband. He had only stood by while the trigger was pulled, but the other man had vanished. The newspaper called him a "child of the forest" and said that the judge's words had to be translated to him through an interpreter. Oscar was sentenced to be hanged on September 18, 1875. Newspapers described the dramatic scene: "The poor mother stretched her arms through the bars and with heartrending sobs pressed her face to that of her boy through the little square aperture, shrieking for mercy and declaring him innocent. Oscar's heart softened and his eyes filled with tears. The mother threw herself upon the breast of the marshal and implored him, for God's sake to save her son. It brought tears to many eyes."

Application for pardon was made, and the sentence was commuted to life imprisonment. Snow begged to be hanged, saying he would rather die than remain a prisoner for life. After five years, the warden of the Joliet penitentiary reported the prisoner's conduct good, and the president of the United States granted a pardon.

Women in the News

A female convict gave birth to a baby in November 1875. She had been in the prison for only two months. By the end of the month, it was reported that the youngster had a new cradle and often made himself heard.

Kankakee County had the distinction of sending the first woman to prison on a life sentence in Illinois. Wilhelmina Took and Peter Wermemont, her paramour, were sentenced in 1876 for murdering the woman's husband. There were only twenty-four female prisoners at the time. They were confined on the top floor of the main building in comfortable quarters, which they had decorated with flowers and pictures cut from papers. They were kept busy repairing the clothes of the inmates and putting toes into machine-made stockings.

Guards

According to the *Joliet Weekly Sun* of December 2, 1875, "Much depends on the character of guards and officers in successfully applying means most conducive to general results of good in prisons."

The guards pose with their canes. *Courtesy Will County Historical Museum and Research Center.*

Christmas Services

At the close of 1875, it was reported that work was suspended on Saturday at noon and Christmas would be celebrated on Sunday in the chapel. One of Peoria's leading businessmen, a popular citizen, prominent Christian and the "prisoner's friend," gave an address along with the chaplain. The choir sang. The warden delivered a brief address "in his usual elegant, graceful easy style; the address contained some sound, practical counsel, and made a visible impression—as his remarks always do on the minds of the convicts." He then presented a pardon on behalf of the governor to William Butler. The *Joliet Weekly Sun* reported: "Butler was overcome with emotion and wept for joy. When he walked up the aisle to receive his pardon, he tottered and trembled like an aspen leaf. He is a negro and was sent from Cairo in '66 for murder for life. He was chief cook for the Warden seven years. For the last year or two he has been cook for the hospital. He was an exemplary convict, never having been reported, reprimanded or even reproved....The convicts' Christmas dinner was rich and abundant, consisting of potatoes and turnips boiled and mashed and richly seasoned, pickles, roast mutton, and bread and coffee with five apples apiece. It was indeed a merry Christmas."

AN ACCOUNTING OF PRISON PROVISIONS

At the top of 1876, the *Joliet Weekly Sun* listed the amount of provisions, meat, breadstuffs, vegetables and other items consumed at the prison.

> *It entailed every day about 1,200 pounds of meat, beef and pork; 13 barrels of flour; 50 pounds of coffee; 30 bushels of potatoes; 7 1/2 bushels of beans; and a large amount of onions and cabbage.*
>
> *On Sundays, 1,500 pounds of roast beef is used; Mondays, 1,500 pounds boiled beef; Tuesdays, 900 pounds stewed beef with soup; Wednesdays, 1,500 lbs. Roast; Thursdays, 750 pounds stewed and soup; Fridays, 1,500 boiled; Saturdays, 750 pounds with soup. 8,000 pounds of beef per week, 210 bushels of potatoes, 91 barrels of flour, 450 pounds of coffee and 60 bushels of beans, besides a large quantity of butter, lard, molasses, spices, etcetera.*
>
> *There was used last year 77,000 lbs. of beef, 65,000 lbs. pork; 8,000 lbs. hams and shoulders and a large amount of chickens and turkeys; 4,368 bbl. Flour; 10,080 bu. Potatoes; 31,200 lbs coffee; 2,800 bu. Beans; besides large quantities of sugars, syrups, fruits, sauces, spices, etc.,—the cost was enormous. Mr. Dempsey, who had been the prison butcher for ten years was packing beef for summer use. Sixty head were slaughtered every week. Mr. Dempsey understood his business and meats packed by him always kept perfectly, never tainting or spoiling.*

ELECTRIC ANNUNCIATORS IN THE WARDEN'S HOUSE

In March 1876, call bells were installed throughout the apartments of the warden's house. The bells worked on the same principle as telegraphic instruments, the clapper of the bell serving as the key of the instrument. The bells in the various rooms were connected with a battery in the chief clerk's office by fine insulated copper wire running both to and from the bells, making a complete electric circuit. Both key knob and annunciator are required, the same as in a telegraph, to receive and transmit calls or messages.

These instruments were being introduced into all the leading hotels and banks in the country. They were manufactured by Whitmore, True & Company of Cleveland, Ohio. The first name in the firm's title belonged to a brother of Sidney W. Whitmore, the assistant clerk and telegraph operator at the prison. He suggested the electric alarm be introduced at the prison. The benefits of the system were immediately recognized.

If the warden desired to see his deputy, he simply touched a key and the announcement was instantly made in the deputy's office that his presence was required in the warden's office. If visitors presented themselves desiring to see the warden, the clerk didn't have to interrupt him but touched the key of the instrument on his desk and the warden was made aware of the fact. If engaged, he transmitted back immediately, "engaged"; if not, "admit them." By this alarm, connected as it would be with every sentry box, turret and shop as well as all the offices in the prison, no escape or trouble could occur at any point without it being instantly known to everyone on the prison premises and indicating the precise place where the trouble was taking place.

Intended to Kill

On March 16, 1876, the keeper of the shoe shop, a Mr. Boaz, was taking down the names of those who had reported sick. A convict approached the keeper's desk. Boaz supposed that the convict wanted to talk to him and kept writing out his sick list. Boaz intended to give him his attention when he'd finished the task. When he was only two feet from the desk, the convict hurled a piece of iron at Boaz with great force. The blow struck him on the head, cutting a deep gash on the right cheek at the base of the nose and fracturing the upper maxillary. There was no question that the convict intended to kill the keeper. He had been acting strangely of late, and it was thought that he would be pronounced insane by the physicians. If not, it was probable that an action would be taken against him for assault with intent to kill, which would add five or ten years to his time in prison.

The Praying Band

In August 1876, the *Joliet Weekly Sun* reported that the Joliet Prison chaplain's labors were met with abundant success. Scarcely a Sabbath passed without a number of inductions to his class—the Convicts' Religious and Mutual Help Society, or "Praying Band." Outside ministers often helped him in the outreach with great success. Most of the convicts were very sincere in their professions of conversion, repentance and change of heart. Though some more hardened and skeptical convicts ridiculed them, many repented and openly resolved to serve God.

ESCAPE FROM THE ICE POND

In late October 1876, a gang of fifty short-time prisoners were employed on the ice pond nearly a mile east of the prison. These convicts were under the charge of a keeper and three armed guards. The labor consisted in pumping the water from the pond preparatory to cleaning it out to be refilled and to produce ice for the prison's use the next summer. As the keeper was lining the prisoners up to march them to the prison, six of them sprang from the line and ran at top speed, four going north and two south. The guards could not leave the main gang to pursue the fleeing convicts but held the ones that were left while they kept up a brisk fire at the fugitives. Two of them fell but got up and kept on, one of them leaning against the fence as he ran. When the news reached the prison, it was too dark to make a successful pursuit. The next morning, the deputy warden and several officers were on the trail by daylight. The warden joined the pursuit on horseback after telegraphing in every direction to head them off. Saturday afternoon, three of the convicts were recaptured near Blue Island station. They had on citizens' clothes, which they had stolen some time during the night. A telegram notified the warden at noon the same day that another of the escaped prisoners had been captured in Chicago. Officer Hall was dispatched for him and returned with the runaway in the evening. This one, also, had on a very genteel suit of citizen's clothes. The other two were still on the run.

A march through the snow. *Courtesy Will County Historical Museum and Research Center.*

The Lincoln Body Snatchers

James Kinealy owned a saloon in Chicago, which was a front for a successful counterfeit money operation. His profits were fantastic, until disaster struck. Benjamin Boyd, the master engraver, was arrested and sent to prison. In June 1876, Big Jim evolved a plan to get Boyd out of the penitentiary in Joliet, Illinois. He recruited Terence Mullen and Lewis G. Swegles to help him steal the body of Abraham Lincoln. The plan was to get the body from its burial place in Springfield, carry it in a wagon to the sands near Lake Michigan and hide it. A deal would be made with the governor of Illinois: the ex-president's corpse in exchange for the governor's pardon of Boyd and a pile of gold.

On the night of November 6, 1876, the men sawed the padlock off the iron door at the burial place, pried off the marble lid and lifted Lincoln's wood casket out. Swegles went to get the wagon and returned with eight Secret Service men. He had served two terms in the Joliet penitentiary, but he was not a grave robber. He was an informant for the Secret Service. The agents rushed in, but the robbers had gotten nervous and fled. Ten days later, Kinealy and Mullen were caught in Chicago. Though the American public was outraged, there was no law against stealing a body. Kinealy and Mullen were sent to Joliet for a year for conspiring to steal a coffin worth seventy-five dollars.*

Mollie Brown's Desperate Attempt at Escape

Twenty-nine-year-old Mollie Brown had come from New York to Chicago, where she was arrested for larceny and sentenced to three years. She had not been in prison a week before she was raising Hades in her surroundings and was constantly scheming some manner of escape. Several months after her arrival, she received a visit from a man passing himself off as her brother but who afterward proved to be Bill Kay, a noted confidence man with whom she had formerly lived. Their visit lasted only thirty minutes, but during that time, Ray managed to give her a fine steel saw, and a plot was formed for her escape. It was not long before Mollie put her plans into effect. She grossly insulted the matron; as a result of such conduct, she was placed in the punishment cell, which at the time was located in the

* Taylor, "How 'Grave' Mistake Sealed Fate of Lincoln Body Snatchers," *Pittsburgh Press*.

northeast tower of the building. At one side of the dark cell was a small window, some fully seventy feet from the ground, that was protected by two iron bars. Ray had instructed her to saw off the bars of the window, make a rope from her bedclothing and lower herself from the window to the roof of the cell house, thirty-two feet below, where he would be waiting to meet her and assist her to the ground. She later said that before she began her descent from the tower, she knelt and prayed. It was her intention to make good her escape or be killed in the attempt.

It was a cold November night, and Brown was clad only in a thin gingham dress. She crawled through the opening she had made in the window and ventured down the fragile rope she had made from strips of the sheets taken from her bed. She at last reached the end of the rope, and her feet were still treading on air. She looked and realized that she was already below the cell-house roof. It was above and some six feet to the left. Below her yawned the fearful blackness of the prison yard, with its rough stones. A fatal mistake had been made in supposing the roof to be directly beneath the window of the punishment cell. The daring woman made a frantic effort to climb back up the rope to the window, but at that instant the rope loosened, and she fell to the pavement below. Her screams aroused the night guards, who came rushing into the yard and found her a mass of blood and broken bones. They carried her back to the women's department. Both of her legs were broken, and she was injured internally. No one expected her to live, but she did. After remaining in bed for over a year, Brown completed her term but was crippled for life.

Jobs for Ex-Cons

In February 1877, the House Committee on Penitentiary met and discussed the creation of a labor bureau to secure employment for the ex-convict as he comes back again into the world. The warden said that the ex-convict, as he goes out the front door of the prison, seems perfectly lost, especially if it is the first offense. He is thoroughly aware of what crime has brought him to and resolves to be a better man. But he finds that he is behind the times and that the world has gone on, as if he had stopped. He is not prepared to meet the world. He finds his way downtown, he meets those worse than he is, who entice him into the saloon. He soon spends all of his money on drink, and then he starts out to seek employment. After meeting with refusal after refusal, the question occurs to him, "Shall I starve or steal?" He chooses the latter and soon finds himself back within the walls of the prison. Robert McClaughry argued that it would be a great savings to the state if such a bureau was established.

Off to the Circus

In March 1877, a convict employed as a waiter in the penitentiary dining room escaped dressed in citizen's clothing. He managed to procure the garments during the day and at nightfall walked out the main entrance. He successfully passed the guards, who assumed he was a visitor. He made his way to the Michigan Central yard and became dazed. By this time, the prison guards were swarming the city and had finally surrounded the Alton track yard, supposing the prisoner to be concealed among the cars. Finally, the Alton railroad police officer nabbed his man near the depot, at about 8:00 p.m. The prisoner made a desperate effort to escape but was unsuccessful. He was returned to the prison. The prisoner was once a well-known circus performer and athlete. He intended to escape and join the John Robinson Circus. He would probably do his circus business in stripes for about ten months to come.

Frank Rande

In 1877, Frank Rande, the "Brilliant Bandit of the Wabash," had a record of thirteen murders to his credit. A furious demon, Frank caused so much trouble that he frequently made headlines in the local newspapers. When Rande resisted arrest in a pawnshop, an officer was killed in the shootout. He had already been in jail in St. Louis and Galesburg when he arrived at Joliet. He had written several hundred sheets of paper he said was his autobiography. He handed this to the warden with a demand that it be kept safely until such time as he arranged for its publication. Major McClaughry remarked that all necessary data regarding the prisoner's life, convention, career in the prison, etcetera would be kept by the bookkeeper in the regular manner prescribed by law.

Rande became violent when his trash was thrown into the stove and spent three days in solitary as a result. He was put to work in the harness shop, having worked at that trade when he was a younger man. He stayed on track and behaved himself for about a year. One day, the men were being marched to their cells for dinner when he suddenly jumped from the ranks, waved his hat and yelled for the men to come on. He supposed in his vanity that they would follow the lead of such a notorious bandit and dead shot, but they looked at the cold, pitiless muzzles of the Winchesters, each good for sixteen shots, and not a man moved.

Rande was taken away snarling, biting and kicking to the solitary. He came out a changed and subdued man. After that, he was one of the best-behaved prisoners within the walls. He was engaged in the finishing of ladies' sidesaddles and did the work with deftness. He invented beautiful designs in fancy stitchwork. His work was very much appreciated by the foreman of the department. Rande also turned his leisure hours to the invention of a gun, but no one was worried, as the invention was not in a very advanced state.

Rande remained in prison for seven years, and then he attempted to add another victim to his long list. One Saturday morning, he knocked down a guard—Deputy McDonald, whom he blamed for his last stretch in solitary—with a heavy poker in the prison harness shop. This blow alone could have killed the officer, but Rande then advanced on him with a knife to finish the job. He would have killed the guard were it not for another convict, William Raab. Raab threw his arms around Rande, lifted him high in the air and threw him halfway across the shop. Raab then clutched Rande's throat, threatening to choke the life out of him. Convicts with knives and hammers gathered around, yelling for Raab to kill Rande or let them have a chance at him. Guards arrived on the scene and ordered Raabe to let Rande up so they could take him to solitary. But as they passed a workbench, Rande caught up a hatchet and aimed a blow at an officer. The man hit Rande in the face with his heavy cane, driving Rande into an insane rage. He struck right and left with the hatchet at both convicts and officers. Ed McDonald, the deputy warden's brother, entered the shop with a revolver and shot at Rande, hitting him behind the ear. He fell to the floor as if dead but revived when he was taken to the hospital. From there, he was taken to solitary.

After a week of silence, Warden McClaughry paid a visit to his cell and conversed with Rande for a few moments. It seemed that Rande was glad to see him, but later he asked the warden to take him out and hang him in the yard. When his supper ration was brought that evening, Frank was said to be pacing up and down his cell, talking wildly to himself. The supper was placed inside the door and the cell door locked.

On the morning of March 7, 1884, Keeper McDonald opened the cell door to find Frank Rande hanging from the bars. He had fastened his undershirt and suspenders to the top bars of the door and stood on his cell bucket to gain leverage. His pantaloons were placed under the bucket to deaden the sound of his struggles while dying. The headline in the *Joliet Daily News* simply read, "Kicks the Bucket." The story under it said that the people of Joliet could now congratulate themselves over the end of the murderous career of the wretch.

Deputy McDonald recovered from the cruel blow dealt him by Rande and later carried around in his vest pocket a piece of his own skull the size of a half dollar as a reminder of when the greatest desperado Illinois had yet produced attempted to brain him with a bar of iron. William Raab's sentence was commuted by the governor to reward his bravery in saving the life of the deputy warden.

Reverend Murderer McGhee

On June 22, 1877, Sheriff Hills of Dixon brought the wife-murderer Reverend McGhee to begin serving his fourteen-year sentence. He was immediately assigned to the prison harness shop, though the barbed fence contractors and others wanted him. Along the road from Dixon to Chicago, large crowds gathered to see the wife-murderer, and he seemed to enjoy the demonstration made on his account. He stared at the crowd and made such remarks as "hope they'll know me when they see me again." Probably not, as he was soon shorn of his long whiskers, his hair was cropped short and he was clothed in prison stripes.

Stop the Train!

In June 1877, a party of thirteen prisoners destined for the penitentiary were being conveyed to Joliet on the northbound train of the Chicago & Alton Railroad when one of them leaped from the car. The train was stopped, and after considerable trouble, the deserter was recaptured and safely delivered to the prison.

The Fourth of July

In 1877, the glorious Fourth was celebrated at the prison. A heart-stirring address was followed by a quartet singing "The Star-Spangled Banner." From the eyes of some men streamed tears of joy as they went about shaking

Movement within the prison was tightly controlled. *Courtesy Will County Historical Museum and Research Center.*

Men looked forward all year to the Fourth of July, when they were given a little taste of freedom and a couple of cigars. *Courtesy Joliet Area Historical Museum, Illinois.*

hands and clasping each other in their arms. It made the audience realize as they had never realized before how sweet was liberty. Then came dancing, singing, speeches, footraces, football games, athletic contests and the playing of banjo and tambourines. They seemed like a parcel of schoolboys spending recess after long confinement. White and black, old and young alike entered into the full spirit of the hour. At the ringing of the bell from the speaker's hand, the men formed in platoon as if by magic, and in thirty seconds they were again in marching order, forming into line to return to the cell houses.

In the afternoon, the convicts in the female prison were taken out under the charge of Mrs. J.E. Judson, the matron, to the lawn in front of the prison, where they enjoyed themselves in playing croquet and other amusements. After this, they were conducted back to their quarters in the prison, where the pleasures were continued in dancing and music. The Fourth of July celebration was one long remembered by the inmates of the Illinois State Penitentiary as being the most pleasant and most enjoyable ever witnessed at that institution.

Kiss Me, George!

"Kiss me, George!" she said. Though he was chained to the rest of the gang, George managed to kiss the girl. The other prisoners looked on in envy, and the sheriff looked on indulgently. But how much more the prisoners would have envied that kiss, and how sternly would the officers have prohibited it, had either known that, between those coral lips, there was a small key fitting the steel bracelets on George's wrists. Precisely how he put to practical use that farewell kiss is not known, but he soon unlocked his bonds. He bounded through a window of the rapidly moving train and escaped.

A Dangerous Convict

In July 1877, a great conspiracy was formed among the convicts at Joliet Prison. The warden and deputy were to be killed. A fire was to be started in the brush shop, then a rush was to be made on the east gate. Adam Clay was the ringleader, assisted by Ziegenmeyer, the Gumbleton murderer; Mike Rick; James Tracy, later hanged in Chicago; and a dozen others. A trusty gave away the plot to Warden McClaughry. The conspirators were seized and placed in irons. Fourteen of them were given ten days in the solitary.

After Clay was transferred to Chester Penitentiary, he attempted to scale the stockade and was shot down before he could make his escape. He would eventually do seventeen years at Chester and four terms at Joliet in all.

A Stressful Swim

In late October 1877, a convict named Wright attempted to escape from the garden in front of the prison. He swam the canal safely, though several revolver shots were fired at him. Under the persuading influence of several rifles, he was induced to halt and was soon brought back to his old quarters and to solitary. He had less than a year to serve.

Oh, Deer

In December 1877, the pet deer that had been kept in the solitary yard at the prison became completely unmanageable. He had been fed by a lifetime prisoner but had recently attacked his keeper in a savage manner, nearly killing the poor fellow. Constable William Pelkey shot the "game," and the carcass was taken to Fred Rapple's market, where it was cut up and sold. The proceeds of the sale were distributed among the poor.

Convict No. 2854

Frank Johnson, convict no. 2854, escaped from the penitentiary in March 1878 while at work in the cooper department outside the east gate. He went to Montana and then to Waterloo, Iowa, where he performed some crooked work and was running on a charge of burglary. He was convicted and sentenced to the prison at Anamasa for one year under the name of Frank Foster. During his imprisonment, a plan was laid among him and eleven others, working in the stone shop, to make a break for freedom. When the day came on which they were to make the attempt, ten out of the twelve started, Johnson being one of them. The prison was partly enclosed by a board fence, and for this the ten made a break, taking along with them stone axes to use in cutting through. Two were killed by the wall guards before they got out, and two others were shot after they got outside. The others were all captured and brought back. After this, convict no. 2854 was taken to Fort Madison to serve out the remainder of his time. When that expired, Officer Cronin was on hand and identified him as Frank Johnson. He kindly and gently broke the news to him that he was wanted at Joliet to serve out an unexpired sentence, and soon Johnson was back behind bars.

THE NEW SOUTHERN ILLINOIS PENITENTIARY AT CHESTER

At the end of March 1878, about two hundred prisoners in striped uniforms were taken to Chester, the location of the new southern Illinois penitentiary. They were moving to Randolph County, in the southern part of the state, to make a home for themselves—literally. All of the original buildings were constructed by prison labor.

JUG HANDLE JUSTICE

Robert Sterling, in *Joliet Prisons: Images in Time*, writes the following:

> *In 1878, a prisoner named Gus Reed died while being punished in the solitary unit. Standing handcuffed to a cell door, he became so loud and unruly one night that a guard gagged him to keep him quiet. At the inquest, the guard testified that he was acting on instructions from his superiors. The guard had made the gag from a piece of broomstick and placed it in the convict's mouth. A strap was attached to both ends and cinched tight behind the inmate's neck. When Reed continued to make noise, the strap was tightened until he stopped. On the day of Reed's death, the guard testified that he had flogged the man once and gagged him three times. Prior to using the whip, it was soaked in water to increase the stinging effect of the lashes.*
>
> *The warden, deputy warden, prison physician, and other ranking officers denied ordering any such punishment, especially the whipping. The verdict of the coroner's jury was that the deceased had died from pulmonary apoplexy caused by persistent yelling with a gag in his mouth. Prison commissioners who investigated the death exonerated the warden, gave a mild reprimand to other prison officials, and fired two guards. Under the heading "Jug Handle Justice," a Joliet newspaper complained that, as usual, guards were "made the scapegoats of their superiors who ordered the punishment."*

The Penitentiary Physician

In November 1878, a change was made in penitentiary physician. The fourth year of Dr. A.W. Heise's term as prison physician having expired, Dr. M.R. Campbell was appointed to the position. Dr. Heise had filled the position most ably and successfully. Though an average of 1,700 prisoners had been under his charge constantly, the sanitary condition of the prison, under his direction, had been so carefully managed that little sickness prevailed, considering the number huddled together. The doctor's skill and ability as a surgeon was admitted throughout the West; as a physician of undoubted competency and long experience, his reputation was second to none. His displacement, without cause, just at the close of an important election, was an inexplicable mystery and caused indignation among his numerous friends.

Dr. Campbell, the successor to Dr. Heise, however, was well fitted for the position to which he was assigned. He was one of the most popular and successful physicians. For years, he was favored with an extensive practice. No physician in northern Illinois was better qualified for prescribing for the sick in accordance with the most approved rules of the profession.

Recovered from His Swoon

After a short illness in February 1879, a convict suddenly died. The body was taken charge of by the persons whose duty it was to attend to such matters, and in due time, it was placed in a coffin, preparatory to being buried in the prison cemetery. Soon after, a thumping was heard inside the coffin. When the lid was removed, the man was found to be living. He had recovered from his swoon, was released from his unpleasant confinement and was back to filling his place in the gang as usual.

Around the same time, a convict assigned to the shoe shop had by stealth fitted a false bottom to a large shoebox. Into this he crawled, carrying with him provisions for several days. His purpose was to lie concealed until the search for him was suspended and then to make his escape over the wall at night. Two accomplices weakened, and they disclosed the hiding place after a long search had been made. The would-be liberated man was dragged from his place of concealment and placed in solitary.

FAMILY TROUBLES

Elmer Merrill and Henry Heitzman were brothers-in-law, having married sisters. Family troubles arose between Henry and his wife, Dora, and they did not live peaceably together. Dora and Elmer decided between them to kill her husband in order to secure his property. On March 22, 1879, Elmer Merrill shot his brother-in-law to death with a double-barreled shotgun. Elmer was immediately arrested for the murder and confessed to the crime. He was then used as a witness against Dora, and she received sixteen years for her role in the murder. Five months after Dora's incarceration, Mrs. Heitzman gave birth to a little girl. A bright, pretty child, she was a great favorite in the prison. Dora was very devoted to her little daughter, whom she was very anxious to keep with her as long as possible. During her second year, she was given over to a family for adoption. It was hoped that the child would be prevented from knowing where she was born and the disgrace to her mother.

TOBACCO

In April 1879, Jane Crabtree, who had belonged to a gang of counterfeiters, was ushered into the female department of the penitentiary. She carried with her a sack containing clothing and other items. But it also contained something that she valued more dearly than clothing: "tobacco." She had several large plugs of twist tobacco, made from the pure leaf—enough to last her during her term of imprisonment providing she was allowed to use it. She was very much surprised when informed by the matron that she could not use the weed while in prison. She wore a charm around her neck made of weeds and herbs of different kinds; attached to the end were three ten-cent silver pieces given to her by her first husband. This was also taken away from her, and she was informed that she would not be allowed to have it while in prison.

She immediately made a grab for it, saying, "I will not give it to you. I will see the boss first." When informed by the matron, Mrs. J.E. Judson, that she was to have charge of her, she readily yielded and commenced her prison life seemingly with the best of intentions. When asked where she was from, Crabtree replied, "I am from old Kentucky." She looked like it, for she wore a genuine "Linsey-woolsey" dress, such as is read of in days gone by but seldom seen today. She also wore a sun bonnet of the regular southern style. Crabtree also had the southern twang in her way of talking.

EASTER EGGS

For Easter dinner in 1880, eight hundred dozen eggs were cooked and given to the convicts on Sunday morning. This, with other allowances, made for them an unusually good dinner.

RED PAINT

In April 1880, the prison was undergoing the application of a coat of red paint. The cell doors and iron cell houses were being painted red, as were the grated windows in and about the prison. It was quite an improvement over the black paint that had been so long in use.

A RASH ACT

That same month, a one-armed prisoner purposely placed his remaining arm on a revolving buzz saw and was taken to the hospital. A week or two later, he was suffering from a severe attack of lockjaw, a consequence of his rash act, which would doubtless end his inglorious career in crime.

A HOUSE OF ILL REPUTE

John Duitt arrived to start serving his sentence in late May 1880. The African American preacher had been sentenced to ten years for rape. He had arrived in Springfield a short time before from some western town to solicit funds for the building of a church. Having completed his mission, he was about to return to his home. Some people living in Springfield had relatives residing near Duitt's destination. They wished for their twelve-year-old daughter to visit their relatives and entrusted her to his care. He promised to see that she arrived safely at the home of her family. Instead of going to the train, he took her to a house of ill repute and there committed the crime for which he now stood behind the iron bars.

A Thin Disguise

A convict at the penitentiary devised an interesting plan of escape. As a workman in the harness department, he had access to the coloring fluid they used in the shop. He extracted small quantities over three months and dyed his black-and-white-striped blanket. He made for himself a pair of pantaloons. Next, he took two white handkerchiefs and made a shirtfront. He took another one and made a collar and a necktie. He made a cap out of a piece of buffalo skin. He attached the mustache he made to his lip with wax from the harness shop. The convict asked to see the deputy warden, who saw through his thin disguise. The young man was soon stripped of his homemade clothes.

2

DR. THOMAS NEILL CREAM

"The Lambeth Poisoner"

Thomas Neill Cream was sentenced to the Joliet penitentiary for life. He began his sentence on November 1, 1881, but was later pardoned, allowing him to start a whole new chapter of misdeeds. People have made the case over the years that Dr. Cream was Jack the Ripper.*

Cream graduated in 1876 as a full-fledged MD after writing a thesis on chloroform. His criminal career began almost immediately. In Montreal, a fire was discovered in Cream's bedroom in a house on Mansfield Street. The firemen found a body in the doctor's bed that was later said to be a skeleton dressed in clothes. He was suspected of setting the fire, but nothing could be proved.

He was forced to marry Miss Laura Brooks of Waterloo, Quebec, after "basely betraying" her. During the summer of 1876, Cream lived with his wife's parents. They barely tolerated his presence, as he often scoffed at the "wrong" that was done to their daughter. Cream was finally forced out of the house after trying to perform a criminal operation on his unhappy wife. The drugs administered to her were so potent that, although she lived through the winter, she died as a result in the spring of 1877.

The following winter, Dr. Cream traveled to London, England, where he toured St. Thomas' Hospital with other Canadian physicians. One of these

---

* McLaren, *A Prescription for Murder*.

would later testify that Cream's "habits and conversation were of the lowest order. He was a hard, steady drinker, and was never seen in the company of a respectable woman. I heard him boast of robbing a streetwalker of her purse, containing $25."

Over the next three years, three women died from botched abortions and overuse of chloroform while Dr. Cream was practicing medicine in Canada. He escaped conviction and moved to Chicago, where another woman died in 1878. Cream was arrested along with his mistress, Hattie Mack. Her confession contained a particularly revolting description of how Dr. Cream set about and carried out his nefarious work. A legal technicality cleared the doctor, who was released from custody.

Next, Cream tried to levy blackmail against a Chicago pharmacist, Frank Pyatt. A Miss Stack called at the drugstore with a prescription from Dr. Cream. It called for a harmless mixture, which was dispensed. The woman was found dead the next morning. Cream at once called on Pyatt and warned him that the medicine had been made up wrong and advised the druggist to tear up the prescription. Pyatt refused. Cream then wrote threatening letters to the pharmacist and offered to hush up the matter for a price. Cream was arrested for sending improper postal cards through the mail. He jumped his bail and fled to Belle River, Ontario, where he worked for some time as "Dr. Ross."

Before leaving Chicago, Cream had become acquainted with John Barns, a British Labor Party member of Parliament. Cream pretended to be a great chief of the labor party in Chicago and in this capacity became acquainted with Daniel Stott, a station agent of the Northwestern Railroad at Garden Prairie. Stott was a leader in the railway strikes of 1880–81. Cream became infatuated with Stott's wife, and she induced her husband to place himself under her lover's care for the cure of his epileptic fits. By June 1881, Cream had given her two prescriptions to be filled. At the trial, Mrs. Stott swore that Cream took the capsules from her, inserted a white powder and returned them to her. He told her that if her husband was not quiet after one dose to "repeat the dose." Stott took the capsules that evening and in twenty minutes was dead. The inquest showed that the victim's stomach contained enough strychnine to kill half a dozen adults. Cream was charged with Stott's murder and was brought back from Belle River. He was sentenced to life and became convict no. 4374 in Joliet State Prison. Governor Joseph W. Fifer later commuted his sentence.

Over the years, the case has been made that Thomas Neill Cream was the notorious killer Jack the Ripper.* Cream was supposedly in prison in Joliet, Illinois, at the time of the 1888 crimes. He told Scotland Yard that he had been released on July 31, 1891. In an interview on June 26, 1892, Warden R.W. McClaughry said that Thomas Neill Cream undoubtedly served a term in Joliet.

> *Cream was always claiming that he had been convicted on perjured testimony. He was a Canadian, and was continually writing letters to his father, William Cream, a respectable citizen of Quebec, setting up this claim and urging his father to help him. O.H. Wright, a lawyer of Belvidere who had been present at the trial, thought the evidence had been insufficient to warrant a conviction, but that the jury had given undue weight to the fact which was brought out in the trial, that Cream had been convicted of a similar offense in Canada.*
>
> *William Cream, as I gathered from what he wrote me, did not take much stock in his son's claim of innocence. He was willing, if there was any probability that his son's innocence could be established, to furnish money to that end. On August 5, 1885 he placed in my hands $300 to be paid to attorneys in case they should be able to discover evidence to substantiate his son's claim that the evidence against him was perjured and should secure a pardon. Otherwise the $300 was to be accounted for to William Cream. Mr. Wright did spend some time investigating the case but discovered nothing that tended to confirm the prisoner's claim.*
>
> *The money was held by me until February 8, 1888. On that date, the elder Cream having died in the meantime, I received a letter from his executors instructing me to pay $40 of the money to Mr. Wright for his services; to place $60 to the credit of Thomas N. Cream, and to remit the balance of $100 to the executors* [which was done].

---

* In 2007, author Russell Edwards bought a stained silk shawl that had been found with Jack the Ripper's fourth victim, Catherine Eddowes, in 1888. He gave the shawl to Jari Louhelainen, a biochemist at Liverpool John Moores University in the United Kingdom. His 2014 book *Naming Jack the Ripper* named Aaron Kosminski, a twenty-three-year-old Polish barber who was a prime suspect at the time, as the murderer. The scientific results, however, were unpublished, and geneticists couldn't assess the claims without technical details about the analysis of the genetic samples. In March 2019, forensic scientists again announced the results of DNA testing pointing to Aaron Kosminski. This time, though, the supporting DNA evidence was published in a peer-reviewed journal. Critics, however, say the evidence isn't strong enough to declare the case closed. While the DNA matches a living relative of Kosminski to some degree, it can only definitively exclude a suspect (Adam, "Does a New Genetic Analysis Finally Reveal the Identity of Jack the Ripper?").

> *I think Cream did not get a pardon, and that he was still a prisoner there when I ceased to be warden the following December* [1888]. *He was a smart fellow and was well-educated, a man of criminal instincts and propensities. I should have called him a licentious man, and one apt to be in just such scrapes. He had studied medicine, or pharmacy at any rate. When I last saw him, he was a little over 30 years of age, I should say.*

The lawyer who defended Cream later said that Cream studied medicine to acquire all the knowledge he could of anatomy and surgery. He used this knowledge most effectually to confound the doctors at his trial. He also desired to get rid of women who were in a condition in which they were a menace to society. The lawyer had no doubt that Cream was mad, saying that he wondered that more use of the plea of insanity was not made in the trial in London. Thomas Neill Cream, "The Lambeth Poisoner," was convicted of the murder of Matilda Clover by administering strychnine to her. He was hanged on the gallows of Newgate Prison in London on November 15, 1892. His last words were rumored to be "I am Jack the…"

3

JOLIET PRISON IN THE NEWS, *1880–85*

A CHICAGO MORMON

On March 17, 1882, Clarence E. Davis, "the champion bigamist" who appeared to have five or six wives in various parts of America (and one or two in Canada), received a five-year sentence in Chicago. Davis was a traveling salesman for a New York house. In visiting various parts of the country, he met and won the affections of many young girls. He had a wife in Elkhart, Indiana, but married another in Toronto and, when he tired of her, took another at Detroit. Soon afterward, he again went to the altar, in Quincy, Illinois. It was said there were several other forlorn women in various parts of the country who were looking and longing for the return of their darling Clarence, who disappeared so soon after the honeymoon.

MONIKERS AND TATTOOS

In March 1882, a representative of the *St. Louis Globe-Democrat* examined the criminal records of the *National Detective Journal*, in which was published the description and criminal record of every professional thief and swindler in the United States. Many of these criminals had served four or five terms in penitentiaries and had ties to Joliet. Many criminals marked themselves with India-ink devices. In the absence of ink, they frequently used coal dust, which they pricked into the skin with a needle. Though these permanent

A man who tried to escape wore shackles and continued to work. *Courtesy Joliet Area Historical Museum, Illinois.*

marks could aid in their identification, one in every three had them—from a full-rigged ship to a small star or anchor. Billy Forrester, the so-called Nathan murderer of New York, had his body completely covered with designs in colored inks. Detectives didn't know this in 1871, when a large reward was offered for him. At least fifty men were arrested who answered to the published description of Forrester, and every officer was sure that he had the right man.

Some Items of Interest from the Tour of Joliet Prison

The laundry, operated by steam, was equipped with all modern appliances. The library for the use of prisoners was maintained by the fees paid by visitors. In 1882, there were 7,500 volumes of travel, biography and fiction. The chapel was a well-appointed hall in which about six hundred convicts assembled on Sunday afternoons to hear the gospel under the rather chilling presence of thirty guards, each armed with a Winchester. There was a school conducted each evening for the benefit of the wholly illiterate. African American men express much eagerness to learn to read and write and outnumber their white brethren in the class.

"Big John" Dyer

"Big John" Dyer was the second-most powerful, muscular man in the prison. He refused to do any kind of labor. When put in the stone shop to work, he assaulted his fellow convicts. When the superintendent of the stone shop tried to stop him, Dyer chased him with a hammer. The man ran out of the shop and made a break for the warden-house door, some three hundred yards away. The convict chased him, gaining on him as they went. Luckily, Dyer stumbled over a stone pile near the machine shop. A dozen men—convicts and guards—held him down until he was ironed, hand and foot. He was taken to his cell, where he remained for over a year. He wore a forty-pound ball attached to his right leg by a chain ten inches long.

Shot in the Palmer House

In July 1882, Theresa Sturla shot Charles Stiles, caller of the Chicago Board of Trade, which created a great sensation all over the country. She was tried on the charge of manslaughter, convicted and sentenced to Joliet Prison for one year. At the time of her conviction, she announced a determination to reform and lead a virtuous life. She preferred to be known by the name Madeline Stiles, which she used when kept by the love whom she murdered in the Palmer House.

Greased Lightning

A reporter for the *Wilmington Advocate* was on the Denver train going north in November 1882. In the forward part of the crowded smoking car were Sheriff Gill and four assistants, in charge of ten prisoners from Peoria, whom they were escorting to the penitentiary. Among them were the notorious Roan brothers, Frank and Phil, "sent up" for three years and

Coal cars on the lawn southwest of the prison. *Courtesy Joliet Area Historical Museum, Illinois.*

one year, respectively. When the train stopped just south of Joliet, Frank shot headfirst out of the window, struck on his hands and knees and lit out like a streak of greased lightning across the neighboring fields. Before the officers in charge could gather their scattered wits together, the train was moving again so rapidly that they were afraid to jump off and go in pursuit. Frank made good his escape. He had managed, with the assistance of the man who occupied the seat next to him, to get the shackles off his ankles and was consequently entirely free when he made his escape.

November 27, 1882

The *St. Louis Globe-Democrat* of November 27, 1882, included the following report:

> *When people from Joliet are asked the population of the town, they give a number followed by "of course, not including the Penitentiary." There is a great grain elevator here, a large number of mills of various kinds, and the streets present handsome business rows, but the Penitentiary pervades all. The man with the eagle eye and navy-blue coat, whom you meet on the street, is a Penitentiary guard. The chances are that every wagon loaded with groceries or other supplies headed north is going to the Penitentiary. Every train that arrives has shackled passengers, guarded by*

a sun-browned Sheriff and his slouched-hat deputy. When you get on the street cars, one placard requests you to "put the exact fare only in the box, as the driver is not allowed under any circumstances to receive or deposit;" and another informs you that "visitors will only be shown through the Penitentiary at 9 am, 11 am, 2 pm, and 4 pm." The streetcars on the outside are labelled "To the Railroad Depots and Penitentiary." The two men met on the streets, wearing very new and stiff jeans, shirts and coarse black hats, are discharged convicts, with $10 each in their pockets and a railroad ticket to the point from which sent up. They must leave town by the first train. The M.P. in blue uniform will see that they do. When you are introduced to the prominent citizen and have remarked that Joliet seems a most promising town, he inquires with pride: "Have you visited the Penitentiary yet?" Just like in Cincinnati, they ask "Have you seen the fountain?" or in Chicago: "What do you think of our lake?"

A Visit to the Women's Department

In March 1883, a reporter for the *St. Louis Globe-Democrat* visited the prison and described the women confined there:

Alice Murphy is the most notorious of the five colored female prisoners. She killed a white man in Chicago last March, for which she was sentenced to twenty-seven years' imprisonment. Alice is a repulsive looking damsel but is safer behind the bars than she would be outside. It is probable she will serve her full time, as she was a degraded prostitute, with no friends except among that class. Kate Wolff, the shoplifter, whose career of devilment has extended through a series of years, is a hardened criminal. She first became distinguished as an accomplished thief in Milwaukee some time ago, where a big silk and dry goods house was relieved of several thousand dollars' worth of stuff, which Wolff got away with successfully. She had several other exploits afterward but was finally nabbed in Chicago and sent down to Joliet for eight years' recreation. Two women are serving a second term for larceny. Kate Morrissey claims to be a sister of the late John Morrissey, of New York—ex-Congressman and prize fighter. The youngest prisoner is Mary Monk, aged eighteen, a thief from Chicago, and the oldest is forty-four. The convicts are not allowed to converse with each other during the day, but at night they may chat in a low tone from six to nine o'clock.

The female convicts did the laundry and sewing. *Courtesy Joliet Area Historical Museum, Illinois.*

Theresa Sturla, the paramour and murderess of Charles Stiles, was escorted to the penitentiary in January 1883. Within the month, she managed to get drunk in the State Prison and brought a keeper into trouble for allowing her to escape ordinary discipline. She said that she had no further use for philanthropists, such as befriended her during her remarkable trial in Chicago and refused even to see them. One wealthy woman offered to adopt her as a daughter, have her thoroughly instructed in music to develop her wonderful voice, and then put her on the concert stage; Theresa declared that her beauty and notoriety are quite sufficient to make her fortune as an actress, and she "wouldn't bother with studying music."

The hardest part of the female prisoner's life is that she is always shut up, without a chance to exercise in the open air, or bask in the warm sunlight. Only twice a year, on Christmas Day, and some other occasion determined upon by the Warden, do they leave their apartments and enter the precincts of the male prison, where they hear services in the chapel, but in the gallery above the heads and away from the glances of the masculine law-breakers. Perhaps the characters of the women in the Pen are worse than those of the men, but they seem easier to manage. A woman must be a pretty hard case to break into any State's prison when juries and Judges are invariably lenient to an offender of the tender sex, and only those black with crime and utterly degraded are cast into durance vile. The prison authorities have little or no hope of reforming their female convicts, but the best and kindest influences are, nevertheless, thrown around them, which are often repaid with ingratitude or a display of vicious disdain.

A Walk Through the Hospital

The reporter continued his tour through the hospital, where, at the time of his visit, were twenty or thirty indisposed convicts.

Some of them were at death's door, and all were very sick. It is impossible for a prisoner to get into the hospital unless he is really ill. On the first floor of the hospital house is the drugstore and larder. The latter was plentifully stocked with chickens, fruits and other dainties, which are liberally supplied to those whom the physician, Dr. Stewart, thinks would be benefitted by them. On the second floor is the hospital proper, where I found twenty men reclining in various positions. "That man there," said the guard, pointing to a tall, slim fellow coughing violently, evidently in the last stages of consumption, "is William Tarbell, one of the worst highway robbers in the country. He was pardoned out about a year ago to die, but in three months he was sent back again from Chicago, and this time it is likely he will croak here."

The poor fellow looked as though he was about to meet the rider on the pale horse, but the guard uncharitably observed that sometimes these fellows held out a good while. Around the walls were mottoes in colors suitable for sick people, such as "What Shall I Do to be Saved?" and "Perfect Love Casteth Out Fear." The chaplain of the prison frequently visited the sick and tried to point their erring footsteps to the "Lamb of God." Seated in a large armchair, his head reclining upon his breast, was an old man once famous in criminal annals as one of the greatest of counterfeiters—Nelson Driggs. Decrepit with age and broken down in health, he has hardly enough energy left to creep about the hospital and lay himself down to rest at night. He will soon fill a grave in the penitentiary graveyard or furnish material for some medical college dissecting-table. There is something indescribably sad about a prison hospital, and each poor devil found there has some good traits in his character which entice him to a kind word or even a sympathetic tear from the more fortunate of humanity.

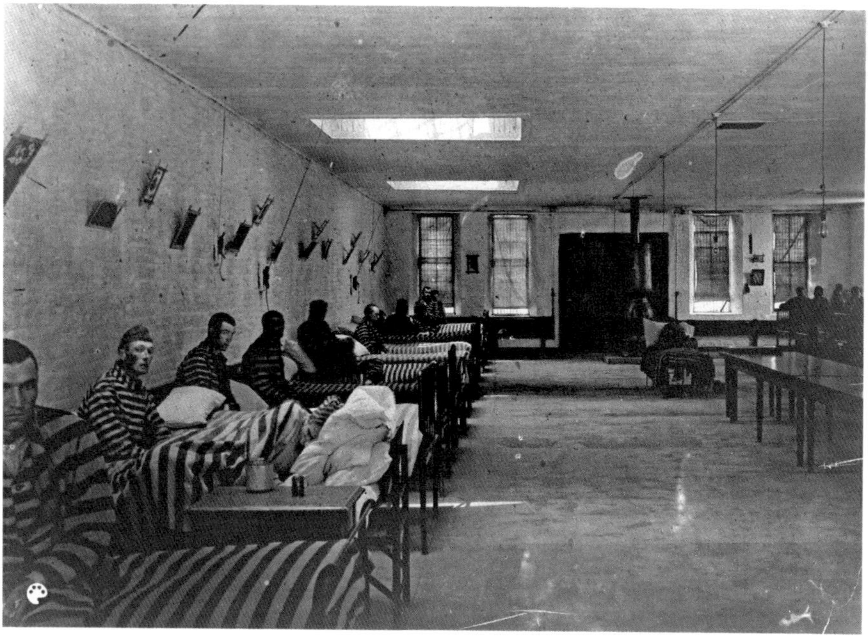

Unsanitary living conditions in the prison drummed up a lot of business for the hospital. Poor ventilation and close quarters were constant concerns. *Courtesy Joliet Area Historical Museum, Illinois.*

Murdered His Cellmate

At about 10:00 p.m. on May 30, 1883, a sudden and awful shriek startled the night watchman, who was softly pacing the corridors of the east prison cell house. When officers reached cell no. 10, Michael Mooney was in his bunk. His cellmate was dead. John Anderson's body had thirty-three distinct cuts and slashes. A half dozen or more yawned open fearfully in the breast, from three to six inches long clear through the body. One cut on the back of the right hip was nearly severing the leg. The hands were cut all over, front and back, and the arms, side and back were stabbed in several places. The throat was cut, and a terrible gash entered the back of the right ear and came out at the mouth, breaking out several of the teeth. A huge knife was found in the cell.

It was uncovered that the two men had been on bad terms. Mooney had said to several convicts who worked near him that Anderson was a cranky sort. He was always asking questions but didn't want Mooney to talk. Mooney told the others that they "needn't be surprised if they saw Anderson carried out some day feet first." Mooney pleaded not guilty.

During the trial, it was brought out that John Anderson had been the only support of a widowed mother. She lay in the Cook County poor farm with no one to look after her. The defense alleged that Anderson had been insane and committed suicide. Mooney, the defense claimed, was awakened from his innocent sleep by the shriek of the frenzied man, who lay on the floor cutting and finally killing himself.

A Baby Boy

In October 1883, a baby boy was born to a female convict named Lily LaFont. The noted Chicago crook had created a sensation at her trial by claiming to be the daughter of a Dublin banker. She was the wife of the notorious Max LaFont, a Chicago thief, who was also incarcerated at Joliet Prison. When told that his wife had given birth to a son, he seemed wonderfully delighted and asked permission to be conducted to the female prison to see his boy. He ascended the four flights of stairs to the female department as proudly as a hero, without a thought of the shame he and his convict wife had brought on the little innocent boy.

A Fire in the Library

In November 1883, the carelessness of a convict caused a commotion at the penitentiary. After lighting the lamps in the library, a match was thrown into a spittoon filled with sawdust, which soon opened the way for a lively blaze. Fortunately, the fire was discovered in time, and the prison fire department soon extinguished it without much damage.

Uncle Tom

Thomas A. McLaurie was a Scotchman and the uncle of Warden McClaughry. For many years, he acted as the assistant librarian of the prison. He was respected and loved by every convict in the prison; they affectionately called him "Uncle Tom." He spent a lot of time doing little favors and acts of kindness for them. After his death, the convicts raised a subscription among themselves for the purpose of perpetuating his memory. They had a suitable plaque made out of black Spanish marble with gold lettering. It was placed on the wall of the prison chapel.

The inscription read:

"I was in prison and ye visited me."
To Uncle Tom
At the earnest request of a large number of prisoners,
This tablet is placed here to perpetuate the memory
Of one whose constant and unwearied kindness
To them gave him the well-deserved title of
"The Prisoner's Friend"
Thomas Alexander McLaurie
Born December 12, 1812   Died May 23, 1883
"After life's fitful fever, he sleeps well."

The following lines were enclosed in convict John Allen's letter to the warden:

In Memoriam

Monumentum Ere Perennius
Above the sleeping prisoners' friend no sculptured pillars rise;
No marble mausoleum, towering to the skies.
Tis but a simple tablet by grieving convicts given,
In loving memory of a friend, who passed away to heaven.

For years his kindness brightened their dreary prison home.
Long—long will live the memories of good old "Uncle Tom."

'Twas not among the rich and proud, his sympathy was shown;
'Twas not in regal palaces "The Prisoners' Friend" was known.
He sought no far-off heathen Good news of hope to tell,
But came in loving charity to the convict in his cell.

Remembering his gentle smile, Like sunshine through the bars.
The convict's prayer for "Uncle Tom" still rises to the stars.
His cheering words, and kindly deeds were given to men whose crimes,
Had made them feared above the savage, in far-off heathen climes.
To desperate men whose bloody deeds had shunned the light of day,
To convicts fettered in their cells, like rending beasts of prey.

To men whose hearts grew hard and fierce, within their living tomb.
Yet such as these were chosen for the friends of "Uncle Tom."
With beaming smile, with good advice, In gentle words of love,
The good old man endeavored, His stubborn friends to move;
And though their brutal tempers were hard as iron to bend,
Deep down within their sullen hearts, they loved "the prisoners' friend."
He needs no mausoleum, no granite sculptured tomb,
Engraved upon their memory, Is the name of "Uncle Tom."
Oxoniesis

THE NINETY-NINE AND ONE

In 1884, there hadn't been an escape from Joliet for some years, though there had been attempts made by some to regain their liberty. A "hide-out" was a common occurrence, but in nearly all cases, the hidden man was found after a brief search. Once, a "cranky" life convict from the Wyoming Territory thought he'd had enough of prison life and would go home. He secreted himself under a heap of rubbish at the foot of the tall chimney that rose from the yard near the machine shops. He covered himself over with old tin cans, bits of paper, barrel hoops and other refuse that had been dumped there.

At count time, a convict was missing from his cell, and as he could not be accounted for, he was put down as a "hide-out." An active search was made for him. After an hour's hunt, the prison guard found him, and he was consigned to the solitary cell. A clever convict who occupied the cell adjoining that of the Wyoming prisoner turned himself loose in poetry over the "crank's" failure to escape. A card bearing the following parody of the famous song of Dwight Moody and Ira Sankey was found in his cell:

There were '90 and 9 that safely lay, in the care of the cell-house guard;
But the one had skipped from the line away, and was "planted" out in the yard.
Away from the keeper's watchful eye, Away from the form of the deputy.
The "count" does show but '90 and 9, "Is that enough for them?"
But the Deputy answered, "One of the line Is 'planted' away from me.
Perhaps he has gone o'er the wall so steep, Or under some building has tried to creep."

Now, none of the other convicts knew The trouble that "crasher" cost;
Nor how closely the workshops were hunted through, Till they found the "con" that was lost;
Hid under a chimney, tall and high, Hungry and dirty and ready to cry.

But hark; there rises a joyful cry—"The missing man is found."
And dark was the frown of the Deputy. When they brought the prisoner round.
But the keepers laughed with might and main. As he went to the "Hole" with ball and chain.

The convict who wrote this poem was without a doubt the best educated inmate in Joliet Prison. Under the alias of John Allen, he was convicted of burglary and sentenced to five years' imprisonment from Champaign in 1882. He was an Englishman who spoke half a dozen languages, French quite fluently. On New Year's Day, while the warden was making a speech to the convicts in the prison chapel, he said he would grant them all permission on that day to write a letter to their friends and requested that each convict write a letter with New Year's greetings to their sweetheart, wife or children.

The next day, the following letter from convict John Allen was handed in to the warden:

To the Warden: In the case of a convict, without either sweetheart, wife or children, alienated from his friends—and far away from home—I presume your request for the writing material, furnished today, to be used will include the "Guardian." In the absence of nearer connections, which I suppose is your position to me—and therefore I write to you. I think the chaplain knows who I am, but although a graduate of Oxford and a medalist of Baliol, with a record of being somewhat of a linguist and mathematician, and of good connections in England, here I am practically without associations, other than criminal ones, which does not come under the heads of the relations you named. Under these circumstances, I write you, as per lines below, and though my "letter" claims no elegance of diction or accuracy, or rhythmic meter, yet I believe that the last line sounds as if it rhymed, without calling in the assistance of the editor. Respectfully, John Allen.

PRISON POETRY

The following lines were found written on a slate in the cell of a recently discharged convict:

Farewell old cell, behind whose grated door I've spent full many a dull and lonely hour; When night, at length, her sable curtain drew Around my cot, well hid from worldly view.
Here, wrap't in slumber's soft embrace, Banished was care, forgotten was disgrace, Until "Old Sol," with radiant luster shone Refulgent splendor on the floors of stone.
Gone are the days when rum, eggnog and punch, Hot rolls or coffee, formed my morning lunch; Or, when dead broke, to get a drink I'd hang Up some bartender with my gift of slang.
Since then, how changed has been my checkered lot—Eggnog and whisky are but things forgot, Bunt coffee pale, bean soup and bread, sausage and hominy now swell my head.
Coffee no more, nor bean-soup twice a week—or other fare—of which I will not speak—Roast beef and corned, potatoes, too, galore; Rump-steak and onions is what I adore.
Even now, I see, as Freedom lifts the veil, Clearly the morn that ends this long travail; then haste sweet day, that dates my exit forth into free air, to value well its worth.
Old friends and pals, here do I now resign; No "hash" hereafter—Number 1769.

FACES OF THREE THOUSAND ROGUES

On January 1, 1884, Warden McClaughry commenced taking the photographs of every new arrival to the Joliet penitentiary. His goal was to make the prison records more complete and furnish a reliable method for future identification of professional criminals and escaped convicts. By August 1886, he had over three thousand portraits.

In the great prison yard stood a peculiarly shaped frame building with a white roof, an object of much curiosity to prison visitors. This building contained two rooms; the front one was used as a loafing-place for extra guards while off duty. The walls of this room were completely covered with thousands of illustrations, cut from such papers and periodicals as *Puck*, the

Joliet Prison was the first prison in the United States to use the Bertillon system of measurement to identify prisoners. *Courtesy Joliet Area Historical Museum, Illinois.*

Judge, *Harper's*, *Leslie's* and other journals. The images were neatly cut and pasted to the wall by an ingenious convict who had charge of the place as janitor and "trusty."

The second room had high, bare, white walls and was without windows except an immense skylight that covered half of the ceiling. This was the prison photograph studio. In this room each convict took his place before the camera. S.W. Wetmore, assistant clerk of the prison, was the photographer who took the convicts' photos. The process in use at the prison was the best that science had yet invented in modern photography. The artist could make the negatives of ninety-eight people in succession without once leaving the side of his camera.

The photo-cabinet in the warden's office contained over three thousand pictures. The faces were a study in human nature—criminals of all ages, from the boy of fifteen to the gray-haired offender of eighty. The sly pickpocket, the dangerous burglar, the scientific safe-blower, the adroit sneak-thief, the clever confidence bilk, the embezzling clerk, the man of too many wives and the red-handed murderer were all there, with sentences ranging from a year to a life term. They all had to face the camera, much against their will, and leave their features recorded there.

In case of an escape, the negative of the fugitive was at once hunted up, and in a few hours' time, several hundred copies of the man's photograph were mailed in all directions for his recapture. When William Pile escaped, he kept in the country and shunned highways and towns until he had been gone several weeks, finally hiring out as a farmhand in central Illinois. One day, his employer directed him to drive the two-horse wagon to the railroad station and get a load of drain tile. Pile went to the station and handed the agent an order for the tile, but the moment the agent set his eyes on Pile, he recognized the man as answering to the photograph of an escaped convict. He drew the picture from his pocket and in ten minutes' time had Pile under arrest. A few days later, the station agent obtained the reward for Pile's recapture.

A BIBLE FOR EVERY PRISONER

A Bible was placed in each cell, according to the rules of the prison, and one could be seen on each self. But as their covers were generally covered with dust, one was inclined to think that they were seldom handled. Besides the Bible, each cell was provided with a catalog of the prison library, from which the convicts made their selections of reading matter. Some of the convicts had quite a little library of their own, consisting of books sent to them by outside friends and others that they had been permitted to buy with money earned as overwork in the various contract shops. A couple of the horizontal wooden labels, containing the names and register numbers of the occupants, were attached to the bars at the top of each cell door.

During the day, when the convicts were in the shops, the cell-house keepers inspected the cells and iron doors of each to see if any mischief had been done. The convicts, in their attempts at escape, sometimes sawed door bars nearly through, concealing the saw cuts with moist bread and soap made into a paste, leaving the final cut until the night they planned to make their escape. The doors were struck sharply with a hammer by the guards, and if the resulting sound had a clear, sharp ring, it showed that the bars were sound and had not been tampered with. But if the door gave forth a dull, dead sound, the watchful guard noticed it instantly and looked for the cause. The cell houses were lighted by gas, and the jets remained burning all night so that the night guards could see every portion of the vast building.

Joliet's Released Prisoners

During the month of May 1884, eighty-two new convicts were admitted to Joliet and forty were released by expiration of their sentences. The newspaper usually printed a summary of the ins and outs, deaths and transfers. In this case, two were sent to the insane asylum and one had died.

One of the most noted criminals to be released that month was the notorious thief and kidnapper "Yellow Sam." In the spring of 1875, Sam was arrested in Chicago for stealing and was given two years at Joliet Prison, where he remained only two months. He made his escape from the slaughterhouse, which was located just beyond the prison walls. Sam had been taken out there to assist the prison butcher in killing a calf. Instead, he sprang through the door and made for the woods. Two years later, Sam was arrested in southern Illinois for burglary and, under the name of Joseph Jeffries, was sentenced to Joliet again. He succeeded so cleverly in disguising his features that none of the keepers suspected him of being "Yellow Sam," the escaped convict. He served his term and was released.

In 1881, he turned up in Indianapolis, where he kidnapped an eight-year-old boy named Adolphus Williams, taking the child to Richmond, Indiana. There, Sam also got hold of another little child named Willie Ratcliffe. He compelled the boys to walk over the rough and frozen roads through Indiana and Ohio. When their feet became sore and bruised from their long walk, their abductor would whip them with a piece of rope to make them continue. Camping in the woods at night, the convict would tie the boys with rope so they could not escape. During the day, he made the boys beg food from farmhouses along the way, threatening them with death if they cried or complained about their treatment.

Near the outskirts of Troy, Ohio, the escapee and the boys were overtaken by a marshal who had been on their track for a week. Sam fired two shots at the officer but was apprehended. The children, who were nearly dead from starvation and cruel treatment, were cared for by kind people until their parents were notified. Sam was sentenced to three years at the Jeffersonville Penitentiary. The authorities at Joliet learned through a letter from a convict in Indiana to one confined at Joliet that the Indiana abductor, Walker Amos, was none other than "Yellow Sam," the escaped convict. A description of the man was received from the warden at Jeffersonville, and when the abductor's term expired in that prison, a detective from Joliet was on hand to take him in charge. When Amos reentered the prison, he created a sensation among the prison keepers by confessing that since his escape in 1875 he had been sent back to the prison under the name of Joe Jeffries and served two whole years without any of them knowing that he was an escaped convict. The records were examined, and his statement was found to be true.

TEMPERANCE WORK

Wednesday, June 9, 1884, was appointed as a day for temperance work in the state prison. On that day, women brought flowers to the prison, which stood as a monument of sin and desperation. The prisoners were shown that there was something better than life within the prison walls.

A PRODIGAL SON

John Kelly was despised by his fellow prisoners, who would lynch him if permitted. His cellmate, John Gaines, was but seventeen years of age when he received a five-year-sentence for his first offense. He was said to have fallen in with bad associates. The two men worked in shoe shop no. 3, Kelly at the bench and Gaines as an accountant. They had been feuding for months. Other convicts had heard Kelly threaten Gaines's life and wanted to speak to the warden about it. Gaines begged them not to, as Kelly would execute his threat. One of the convicts said that Kelly had made revolting propositions and feared that Gaines would report it.

In December 1884, a night guard responded to screams for help and found John Kelly and John Gaines in a desperate struggle. Kelly had dealt his victim a terrible blow on the head with a hammer and then stabbed him twice, breaking the knife blade the second time and inflicting a horrible wound in the abdomen. It was thought that the boy would have been stabbed many more times if the blade had not broken. It was feared that inflammation and blood poison would soon end his life.

Gaines was lying in the prison hospital when his mother and brother arrived in response to a telegram sent to Brooklyn. It seems that Gaines was the son of cultured parents who had lost track of him; they first discovered their son was in prison through the telegram. When the mother's eyes first fell on the pale, prostrate form of her son on the hospital couch, she burst into tears and fell on her knees at his side and exclaimed, "Oh, my boy—my poor boy." The meeting of the mother and son moved to tears the officers who witnessed it. The anguish of the brother, a prominent businessman in Brooklyn, was plainly depicted on his face. They would remain and if possible, nurse the unfortunate young man back to life, though his condition was critical.

Old-Timer's Postcard

In 1885, an "old-timer" who had recently been released sent the warden a postcard on which was written the following:

Discharged again? Yes, I am free; But, Warden, keep a place for me,
For freedom means that I must go; Out in the wind, and rain, and snow,
To fight with hunger, shame and cold; A convict gray, and worn and old.
A new thing, truly, to be free—But, Warden keep a place for me.
For I'll come back, It's seven years; Since first I entered there in tears;
For "burglary and larceny" I came; and felt the burden and the shame,
The prison's taint, the outlaws dread; When first besieged his hopeless tread
The gates clang to with dreadful sound, and the prison walls close round.

"Boston" Thomas

In July 1885, it was reported that seventy prisoners had been received at Joliet from Chicago during the last five days. "Boston" Thomas was again on the list, with his third term at Joliet. During his second term, he was placed at work in the prison stables, located just outside the prison gates and directly under the eyes of the wall guards, who were armed with sixteen-shooter Winchester rifles. One afternoon, a guard was sent out with Thomas and several other convicts to feed the stock. While the guard was in the corn bin measuring out the feed, Boston slammed the door and fastened it, imprisoning the keeper. He then sprang through the stable door and made long jumps for tall timber. Guards opened fire, but without effect. That night, he broke into the residence of the Reverend John White, an Episcopal minister. He fitted himself out with a suit of minister's clothes, taking along a gold watch and a well-filled pocketbook. Thus equipped, Thomas boarded a train on the Rock Island Railroad and made his way to Iowa. Several months later, he was recognized by a Chicago detective walking along State Street. He was captured and returned to Joliet to complete his sentence.

On August 6, 1885, two special cars reached the prison. On board were Jailer Conrad Folz of Chicago and forty-nine convicted criminals. Among the convicts being freed that month was Sadie Ray, who had shot and killed Patrick Kingsley at a hotel in Chicago two years before. Kingsley was the steward of a second-rate hotel, and Sadie was the head pantry girl. "Doc" Newell was also released. Some years before, Newell had eloped with the beautiful daughter of a Boston physician. They fled to Chicago. Newell was sent to prison for burglary. His wife was found later by the police living with a gang of Asian Americans at the opium joint kept by Hoo-Wee-Lee. Mamie was consigned to the Bridewell House of Correction.

The Fairbanks Robbery

The notorious Harry Duncan, alias "Muldoon," was a midnight burglar and masked robber who was sentenced to fourteen years for a robbery at Wheaton, Illinois. Muldoon and two others, all wearing masks, entered the Fairbanks farmhouse at midnight. The womenfolk were tied to their beds, roughly handled and subjected to various cruelties. Mr. Fairbanks was seized, and his feet held over a burning pile of coals in order to torture him into disclosing the hiding place of his wealth, which Muldoon secured, along with a small amount of currency. Muldoon was later traced to St. Louis, where he was arrested. Mrs. Fairbanks was able to identify the man, despite his having cut off his bushy "Dundreary" sideburns. During his incarceration, this desperado, in order to escape from hard prison labor, deliberately chopped off two of his fingers, but even this self-mutilation did not avail him. He was placed in a solitary cell, and when his hand had healed, he was compelled to resume his old place at the beading machine.

The Old Convict Cemetery

"The sentence of the court is that you be conveyed to the penitentiary, and that there you be imprisoned for the term of your natural life." Those are

The old convict cemetery on the hill. The wood grave markers are long gone now. *Courtesy Joliet Area Historical Museum, Illinois.*

If a convict's family did not claim the body, a simple service was performed by the chaplain, and the convict was buried in the old cemetery on the hill. *Courtesy Joliet Area Historical Museum, Illinois.*

the ominous words pronounced by the court. They were supposed to mean an absolute isolation from the outside world as long as the victim drew the breath of life, to be enclosed within four walls, with no hope beyond them, and to feel that there he must remain until death came and carried him out feet-foremost to the convicts' graveyard on the hill. The *Chicago Tribune* on September 28, 1887, called the place "oblivion itself," where all identity was lost. "A nine board stuck here and there" pointed out a grave. Inmates who died before 1925 and were unclaimed were buried at state expense in the old Joliet Prison cemetery. Very few records exist of the men and women who were buried there. The markers were simple wood crosses that decayed long ago.

> *On a woody knoll, half a mile east of the prison, is the convict cemetery. An enclosure of some two acres in extent, completely surrounded by woods. A wagon road starts from the eastern gate of the prison, winds its way across the prison farm and up the stony bluff to the dismal spot. During the past twenty-five years several hundred dead convicts have gone from the prison, feet foremost, incased in plain pine coffins, over this road to an unhonored grave.—Pardoned out of prison by grim death.*

4

THE HAYMARKET ANARCHISTS

On May 4, 1886, seven people were killed and sixty or more wounded by bombs thrown by anarchists in what would become known as the Haymarket Massacre.* The anarchists were members of a revolutionary organization called "The International." For more than a year before, a general strike for eight hours as a day's work had been contemplated. These men had been endeavoring to gather the working classes into ranks and had urged them to arm themselves, especially with bombs. On May 1, 1886, there were many strikes. On May 3, a serious riot took place at the McCormick Harvesting Machine Works. The police used force, and several people were hurt. On the night of the following day, May 4, the anarchists called a meeting in Haymarket Square to denounce the police. The police marched to the meeting and ordered the people to disperse. At 10:30 p.m., a dynamite bomb was thrown into the ranks of the policemen, killing officer Mathias J. Degan and six others. Sixty people were also wounded. The trial began on July 14 and ended on October 9, 1886.

August Spies, Michael Schwab, Samuel Fielden, Albert R. Parsons, Adolph Fischer, George Engel and Louis Lingg were found guilty and sentenced to be hanged, but only three of them actually paid the penalty on the gallows. Oscar W. Neebe was sentenced to fifteen years in the penitentiary. The sentences of Schwab and Fielden were later commuted to life imprisonment. Lingg, by suicide, escaped hanging. On November 11, 1887, the other three defendants were executed.

---

* Green, *Death in the Haymarket.*

The Haymarket anarchists, from *The Pictorial West* of August 1886. *Chicagology*.

On September 27, 1887, Oscar Neebe was quietly transferred to Joliet Prison to "don his stripes." He would begin to serve the fifteen-year sentence imposed on him for his part in the Haymarket conspiracy. Thomas Broderick, the railroad dynamiter, was received at Joliet on May 4, 1889, and discharged on April 3, 1890. He alleged gross cruelty and brutality against the prisoners, especially Fielden and Neebe. The allegations were stoutly denied by the prison officers and denounced as a pack of lies by the convicts.

In June 1892, it was reported that societies in Chicago were organizing a movement to secure a pardon for the three Haymarket anarchists at Joliet. In October, the Amnesty Association announced that the petition for the pardon of the "Haymarket Anarchists" would be held off until after the November elections. This was requested by Fielden, Neebe and Schwab so that it could not be used for political purposes.

On June 26, 1893, Samuel Fielden, Michael Schwab and Oscar Neebe were freed. Governor John Peter Altgeld pardoned them, declaring that their conviction was unjust and illegal. E.S. Dreyer returned from Springfield to Warden R.L. Allen at Joliet at 4:00 p.m. with the letters of their deliverance. The three men were brought in to meet with the warden, all wearing the striped garb of penal servitude. When given their papers, the men shook hands with Dreyer and the warden. They were given suits of clothes and congratulations. Two hours later, the men took the train to Chicago. They returned quietly to their homes without demonstration of any kind. The papers told of joyful reunions at each man's home.

5

JOLIET PRISON IN THE NEWS, *1885–97*

MISSION DAY

June 9, 1886, was declared Mission Day at the prison. The ladies of Joliet arranged bouquets for the prisoners. A Bible verse or card containing words of counsel was tied to each of the 1,550 bouquets. The ladies thought that if only one of those sin-defiled men or women could be turned to a better life, they would be paid for all their labor. They hoped that many of them saw that the hand of God was in the work. The ladies were taken up into the women's department, and there the chaplain gave a short talk to the convicts, urging them to accept the gifts in the spirit in which they were given.

CATHARINE SANTSCHI

In February 1887, Gottlieb and Catharine Santschi were indicted for inhuman treatment of their ten-year-old son. The evidence showed conclusively that the parents had inflicted the most heartless punishments on their helpless child for the slightest offenses. The child's hands had been held on the hot stove until they were burned. He had been beaten until his back was covered with sores. He was strapped to the floor at night during the cold weather of January with no covering. He was kept in that condition until his feet were frozen. His feet had been amputated about a month before the trial. He was so weak and emaciated that an improvised bed had to be prepared for his use while giving his testimony.

There was scarcely a dry eye in the crowd when the little fellow was carried into the courtroom that afternoon to testify against his parents. He told his story through an interpreter (the Santschi family were German) in a straightforward and impressive manner. The child's testimony corroborated that of the other witnesses and made a very strong case against the parents. The parents appeared to be affected not in the least when the child was brought into court, and it was said that they were anxious only as to their own fate.

A reporter for the *St. Louis Globe-Democrat* visited the women's prison on September 10, 1893, and interviewed the inmates there. One of the women was Catharine Santschi.

> *It is almost impossible to believe that some of the women are guilty of the heinous crimes of which they are accused. There is one woman—a motherly looking old soul with parted gray hair and knotted, wrinkled fingers. A swiss woman named Catharine Santschi. With her husband's assistance, nearly tortured their little son to death, leaving him a helpless cripple. It is said that the woman was more at fault than her imbecile husband, who is also a convict. The boy was beaten until his back was raw. His hands were held upon a hot stove until the flesh burned off. He was strapped to the floor and left uncovered one freezing cold night so that it was necessary to amputate both of his feet. Yet she seems like any other woman and is said to show many traits of tenderheartedness among her sister prisoners.*

WEDDED IN PRISON

An interesting marriage ceremony took place in the visitors' reception room at the Joliet Prison at about 5:00 p.m. on March 7, 1887. Edgar Swain had been serving a one-year sentence for bigamy. He had married Emma Gretchen about four years previously, when she was only fifteen years old. He lived with her for three years, then deserted her and married another woman. He was convicted of bigamy and sentenced to the penitentiary. His second wife then married another man. Emma, who had never been divorced from Swain, resolved to reclaim her recreant husband. She waited until the day of Swain's release and made herself known to the prison chaplain, who accompanied her to the county clerk's office and procured a license. They then went to the prison, and Swain was brought before the woman he had deserted. After a few minutes' conversation, Swain agreed to be forgiven and to marry again. The chaplain at once tied the knot in the presence of a party of visitors who were waiting to be shown through the prison. Swain was a handsome-looking fellow of thirty-three and one of the most expert machinists ever confined at Joliet. His wife gave her age as twenty-two.

Colonel William H. Bolton

William H. Bolton held an important position in the Chicago Post Office until drink and the use of morphine and opium caused him to become a total wreck. He was convicted of misappropriating postal funds, resulting in a two-year term at the Joliet Prison. He was pardoned by President Grover Cleveland in 1887. The document stated that Bolton had maintained good character, was trusted by all and had been exceedingly popular before his arrest. He had bravely and gallantly served his country and freely confessed his crime (making none of the flimsy excuses common in such cases). He was sixty years old and broken in health and spirits, and it was hoped that the pardon would help him to renew his struggle for life and regain his character. As he left the prison, Bolton looked like a new man, with his old military bearing, free from the influence of drink and opium. It was thought that the colonel would return to society a regenerated man and endeavor to regain his former standing.

Warden McClaughry's Thirteenth Year

I consider the protection of society the chief object in imprisonment of the criminal—this object to be attained if possible by such methods of discipline as will teach him cheerful obedience to law and restore him to society a helpful rather than a hurtful member of it.
—Warden R.W. McClaughry, 1886

On July 31, 1887, Warden McClaughry gave an address in the chapel, which was filled with convicts. Officers and visitors were there for the occasion. On the occasion of the thirteenth year of his service, he wanted to review the history of the prison during that period and share some of the lessons he had learned.

McClaughry referred to the fact that the past thirteen years had brought them through the administrations of Presidents Grant, Hayes, Garfield and

Arthur and into that of Cleveland and, in Illinois, the administrations of Governors Beveridge, Cullom, Hamilton and Oglesby. In science, great advancements had been made, notably the discovery of the electric light and the telephone.

The warden honored prison officers of long service and sterling merit. He also shared some statistics highlighting the differences thirteen years had brought. He ended by stating that twenty-four prisoners had escaped during his administration. After the convicts' applause had subsided, he informed them that he had recaptured twenty of them and that three had died, leaving but one still at large. Therefore, he said, it does not pay prisoners to attempt to escape from his jurisdiction.

The warden drew a lesson from the fact that of the 1,253 prisoners present when he took charge, just 10 remained. He stated that of the 1,200 who had gone, the majority were no longer living—showing that the lifetime of an average criminal is bounded by thirteen years.

The assurance that one of his seven termers had for the last four years led an industrious, sober and honest life evoked boisterous applause from his auditors, who seemed to see in that fact a hope for themselves. The warden's discourse was listened to with intense interest by prisoners, officers and visitors. The institution's management was never stronger at that time in the confidence of those under its care, as well as of the people at large.

HALF A LIFETIME IN JAIL

In December 1887, James Leonard was visited at Leavenworth Federal Penitentiary by a reporter from the *Chicago Tribune* to get the story of his criminal career. The burglar and jailbreaker had spent half a lifetime in jail. "He was found to be a very pleasant man to do business with, when surrounded by a warden, deputy, and chief clerk; but for a dark alley and a dark night, one could make a more preferable selection than Mr. Leonard." Bribed with tobacco, the convict talked with the reporter for an hour and a half. He listed dozens of jails and prisons he'd been in—many of them he'd escaped from. The reporter said there wasn't a doubt that Leonard tampered with the truth, but the records showed that he'd been an inmate of all the prisons mentioned. If his stories were true, then at the end of his present term he would have spent eighteen years and six months behind prison walls. He at first would not admit he'd been at Joliet but said he knew Warden McClaughry and described him accurately.

David Parker

On June 27, 1888, a woman came by train from St. Louis to see the warden at Joliet. She told the warden that she had married a man many years before who seemed sober, upright and honest. They lived together happily for four months before he deserted her. Three years later, she received a letter from Iowa; her husband had divorced her. She was relieved and went on to marry a wealthy widower in 1881. They were happily married for six years before the husband died. He left no will. She was left to prove that they had been legally married but had no record to prove the divorce from the first husband, David Parker. She had come to some information that perhaps he had been imprisoned in Joliet. The desk clerk searched the records and could find nothing about the man. The record clerk was summoned. He remembered a man by the name of James D. Paddock who was called David Parker by his fellow inmates. He had escaped in late 1879 by sawing through the bars of his cell. He'd been arrested again in February 1880 and returned to prison, had finished his term and been released. The woman left for Chicago to see the Pinkerton Detective Agency, hoping to find that they knew something of Parker.

Mollie Matches

John Larney was released from a ten-year term at Joliet Prison on October 20, 1888. It was while a boy in New York that he had obtained his nickname: Mollie Matches. There was a celebration of some kind in the city, and Larney dressed as a girl and set out to sell matches. He explored the pockets of the masses, using his basket as a blind. His success was so great that he obtained over $2,000 from the pockets of the crowd and since then had always been known by his nickname. During the Civil War, Larney's patriotism was of so ardent a character that he enlisted in no less than ninety-three different regiments in the states of Ohio, Pennsylvania, Massachusetts and New York, regularly jumping away with the bounty every time he enlisted.

James Burke

James Burke was living among farmers south of the Illinois River. He went to the home of Fritz Peterson and announced that he was William McCormick and had twenty head of steers in his pasture that he wanted to sell. They agreed on a price, Burke was paid and Petersen took possession of the steers. It was only later that Petersen discovered that McCormick was not the man with whom he had made the deal. Burke was later arrested in town for impersonation and sent to the Joliet prison.

A CONVICT'S PLUCK

On January 29, 1889, John Dayton was released from a six-year term at Joliet Prison. He was convicted from Springfield, Illinois, and when he arrived at the prison, he knew no trade. They put him to work as a granite cutter. He soon became so expert at the work that he was able to do the work of three men. The contractor in the department offered Dayton pay for all work he would do over a regular day's task. On his release from prison, he was handed the sum of $531 and was assured that he could make a good living outside the prison walls.

THE MURDER OF DR. CRONIN

On May 4, 1889, prominent Chicago physician Dr. Patrick Henry Cronin disappeared. He had recently criticized the board of the Clan-na-Gael, a political organization formed to promote Irish independence from British rule. Dr. Cronin had raised large sums of money for the organization but was suspicious of the secrecy with which the board administered it. When he accused Alexander Sullivan of embezzling funds, he was marked for death. On May 22, Cronin's body was found in a blocked sewer. Daniel Coughlin, Patrick O'Sullivan and Martin Burke were found guilty and sent to Joliet Prison. O'Sullivan and Burke died in the penitentiary.

WHO MURDERED CLARKE?

On July 3, 1889, restaurant-keeper Frank E. Cowlin was taken to the Joliet penitentiary to identify the man he saw near a drugstore just before Druggist Clarke was murdered. Cowlin and Detective Farrell left for Joliet early that morning. Shortly before 11:00 a.m., they reached the penitentiary and were soon admitted to Warden Berggren's private office. The warden then handed Cowlin a number of photographs taken from the rogues' gallery. Cowlin looked them over, and when he came to the picture of "Dirty Eddie" Foy, he exclaimed, "There—that's the picture of the man I saw that night."

Cowlin was left in the reception room while the officer took a seat in the warden's private office. Foy was sent for and brought into the room. The detective commenced to talk to Foy on a subject entirely unrelated to the Clarke murder. In the meantime, Cowlin was brought into the room and introduced to the warden as "Mr. Smith." The moment Foy's eyes fell upon the form of Cowlin, he turned as white as a sheet, his chin dropped and he trembled all over. Cowlin did not speak to Foy but conversed a moment with the warden and then walked out of the room. The detective then ended his interview, and the convict was sent back to his shop. Eddie Foy was part of the gang that had committed burglaries along the line of the Burlington Railroad from Chicago to Aurora. Foy was arrested and sent up for eleven years. But it was thought that they had also gone into the drugstore to rob the till and Clarke was shot while resisting. Cowlin's identification fixed guilt on Foy almost beyond a shadow of a doubt.

A Trusted Convict

Visitors to Joliet were often startled to see a convict in stripes unattended on the prison grounds. And January 24, 1890, was no different. Robert E. Gick had been sent up eight years before for the crime of murder. He had killed a man who had drawn a knife in a fight. Under the influence of liquor, Gick drew a revolver and shot the man. Though he was one of sixty-one "lifers," he was one of the most trusted and favored men in the prison. When the warden's children would spy Gick down the walk, they would race to surround him, cling to his hands and wait for a turn to ride on his back. When Gick was called to do an errand on the other end of the city, he was allowed to wear citizen's clothing and go alone. He would drive the ladies of the warden's family to the city or take the carriage to the city depot to meet a commissioner. An October 22, 1890 article in the *New York World* reported that "Love Caused His Fall." Gick had given in to temptation and planned to elope with

Robert E. Gick, a trusted convict. He was a favorite of the locals. *Courtesy of Mark Dixon.*

a woman from Joliet. He'd gone back to say goodbye to his friends after a few drinks and ended up in solitary. He had the good wishes and sympathy of every man, woman and child in the city, and had a petition been presented for his pardon, five thousand signers could be obtained in Joliet alone. In 1893, Gick's sentence was commuted by the governor, and he was released. He followed his married sisters to their new home in Grand Rapids, Michigan. He later made his way to northern Wisconsin, where he worked as a cook in a restaurant. In 1907, he was taken with a severe attack of cholera morbus and died after twenty-four hours.

The Ford Murder

On June 24, 1890, a traveling salesman named David Moore was found beaten to death in Ottawa, Illinois. An investigation revealed that a woman named Kate Ford had met Moore that morning and agreed to meet him later in Allen Park. She told her husband about it, and they worked up a plan to rob him. Bill O'Brien was enlisted to help. O'Brien's mistress, Minnie Winterling, came along, though accounts differ as to her supposed role.

When Charlie Ford was arrested, he played it cool but said several things that gave him away. Kate would later say that he was "dumb as an oyster." Minnie Winterling was arrested at the home where she was employed as a domestic. She broke down at once and made a full confession but said that it was Ford who had struck first with the coupling pin. O'Brien continued after Ford dropped it. The next day, William O'Brien was arrested. He was taken to jail but wouldn't talk. He was told of the women's confessions but said he knew nothing about the crime.

O'Brien was sentenced in August 1890 to serve a life sentence at Joliet Prison. He served at hard labor in the cooper shop and later died in prison. Kate Ford pleaded guilty and was sentenced to fourteen years. She served until 1896, when she was pardoned by Governor Altgeld. Minnie Winterling went free. Charles Ford had previously served time at the Joliet penitentiary for theft. The *Streator Times* reported that "Ford was too lazy to work for a longer time than a few weeks or a month in one place, and, like men disposed toward crime, who look upon work as slavery, he cast about him to make a living by his wits. He married Katie Weiner, a loose woman from Spring Valley, not over 20 years of age, and with her as his decoy, began a career of petty blackmailing. He looked for larger game as soon as his plans were matured, and his first victim of size was David Moore."

Charlie Ford was found guilty in November 1890 and sentenced to death. He was hanged on the morning on May 13, 1891. On June 1, 1891, Minnie Winterling was locked up to prevent her from jumping into the Chicago River. She was released from the Kankakee Asylum in September 1897 and taken to the home of her parents, south of Ottawa.*

Life in a State Prison: A Grind of Toil That Goes on Ceaselessly

On September 17, 1890, readers of newspapers across the country were given a behind-the-scenes look at life in the Joliet penitentiary:

> *The majority of convicts are barred from all the world, to see familiar face from year to year, receive no word of sympathy, no word of kindness, with a number of hours allotted for work, but none for recreation and plenty of time to chew the cud of remorse; this is indeed a living death. There is nothing inside the grim, gray walls that excites any other feeling than pity for the army of poor devils who, for offenses against society, are forced to engage in a grind of toil that goes on ceaselessly. The surroundings are cheerless enough, to some almost repulsive, and to one who is accustomed to the fullest liberty in speech and action, they are difficult to understand.*
>
> *A new inmate first passes through the ordeal of the solitary and is instructed in the rules and regulations: his hair is cut short, his face shaved smooth, a bath taken, and he is also vaccinated. After a full description of him is noted down—his weight, height, color of hair and eyes, chest, head, and finger measure, etc. he is assigned to some kind of work, usually a trade. If he has one, which is not often the case, and then the grind begins. Every day is the same, there is no change to relieve the monotony of the convict's existence. It is the same with one as with the other. They are called at six in the morning by the ringing of a bell at which all must rise and prepare for breakfast. At seven they are marched to their various work shops where "ball is played" until twelve; one hour is allowed for dinner, which is eaten in the cells, and at six o'clock they retire again for the night. In the winter, quitting time is regulated by the length of the days, as it is necessary to have all the convicts secure in their cells before dark. At nine*

* Perrot, "A Body Found."

o'clock all must put out their lights and retire. No boisterous language or conversations with a prisoner in an adjoining cell is permitted.

At present there are about 1,400 convicts confined in the Joliet prison. Fifteen of them are women. The number of arrivals averages from forty to fifty a month, and naturally the releases about the same.

A newspaper from the time described life in a state prison as one of unceasing toil. *"Life in a State Prison,"* The Citizen *(Howard, KS), September 17, 1890.*

The discipline is humane but very severe, which of course is quite necessary, and the slightest disobedience is punishable by solitary confinement, where the convict sees no one, is obliged to live on dry bread and water, which is handed him but twice a day, and his bed is the stone floor. After returning from a siege of ten days or so in the solitary, the prisoner would make a very good substitute for a corpse. No matter how refractory he may have been, he is always sure to be very weak and submissive when he returns.

But most of the prisoners are very obedient, and strive in many ways to gain favor with the officers in charge by their good conduct, which is in truth the best method to follow, not alone for his welfare as a prisoner, but such a course is also necessary in order to be allowed the good time which shortens his sentence nearly half. This good time commences with one month off for the first year, two months for the second, three months for the third, and so on until the sixth year, when six months are taken off of every year thereafter.

According to this, a prisoner sentenced to a twenty-year term actually serves only eleven years and three months, and a ten-year sentence would be shortened to six years and three months. Thus, it will be seen that good behavior offers a large inducement. A convict, though, may lose all or a portion of his good time if he proves troublesome to the extent of four punishments.

If one could learn the history of each convict's private life before entering the inside of these prison walls, he would discover that people from all stations in life are here brought together and placed on an equality with each other are treated as such. If investigation could be made, one would find here the preacher, lawyer, doctor, men of education and refinement, clerks, college graduates, and in fact men from all positions in life from the influential politician to the professional burglar or common thief. But even to the most scrutinizing eye, all look alike in their habiliments of striped clothing and no one outside of their keepers could distinguish the red-handed murderer from the once influential and respected citizen whose hand is placed on his shoulder as they march along in the lock step. The professional lawbreaker is largely in the majority, and as a rule gives the most trouble. As a general thing, he is very ignorant, from a literary point of view, although very shrewd in many other respects.

Most of the convicts in for murder are serving their first terms, while those doing time for burglary or thievery are, as a rule, serving the State for the second or third time, and among these are many under twenty-two or twenty-three years of age. Most all are innocent (if one listens to their story), and do not deserve the punishment that is being inflicted upon them, and they generally attribute their imprisonment to a prejudiced jury, perjury on the part of witnesses, or to some unfortunate circumstance.

Chapel services are held every Sunday at ten o'clock. Every convict is at liberty to go if he chooses or remain in his cell. Catholic services are held once a month. A regular chaplain is engaged to conduct the services, and a choir and orchestra of convicts furnishes the music, which is very good, indeed, to say the least.

The prisoners are allowed any of the weekly papers, but no dailies. The papers, as also all the letters received or sent, first pass through the hands of the censor, who clips from them anything which he thinks ought not to be communicated to the prisoners. They are allowed to write once in four weeks, and only one letter at a time. Friends may be seen only once in eight weeks. That each convict is numbered is well understood. When that number reaches 10,000 the numbering commences over again; this took place about the first of January last, and will probably not occur again for twenty-five years.

The convicts are shaved once a week and are treated to a haircut once in two months. Neither is a very pleasant sensation. For a shave, each man lathers himself, rubs it in, flops down in the chair, and in a minute and a half is a shaved man. This always takes place in the workshop. The haircut usually looks as if it were accomplished in the dark with a pair of sheep shears or a saw. A bath is taken once a week in summer and once every two weeks in winter.

Most convicts have, before their first week of imprisonment ends, figured out to the hour when they will be released, and have, perhaps, long before that time arrives, planned more than one course they will pursue when they are free again. A number carry out good resolutions, but a large number somehow find their way back again in the course of time. The release is

always made in the evening of the day before their time expires, when the convict is given a good fair suit of clothes, $10 in money and a railway ticket to the place from whence he came. The clothing with which he arrived has all been burned in the furnace of the engine house. In fact, nothing is saved of what the prisoner brings to the prison, but his watch and jewelry and what money he may have. This he may spend for papers only. Visitors are permitted to pass through the penitentiary any day but holidays and Sundays. The hours for going through are at 9 and 11 am and 2 and 4 pm. Twenty-five cents is charged for admittance.
—J.H.H.

MAJOR MCCLAUGHRY'S NEW PLAN

In January 1891, it was reported that Warden McClaughry had conceived and adopted a new system of punishment that would doubtless provoke extended discussion at the next world's Prison Congress. One day, the sharp-eyed major, detecting one of the inmates in violation of the rules of the shoe shop, picked up a leather sole at hand and treated the astonished offender to a thorough and impressive spanking. The effect was so wholesome and touching that it came to the major as an inspiration that he had stumbled across the ideal nineteenth-century system of punishment.

He adopted the process at once and was charmed with its success. For fear that exaggerated reports of the punishment might reach the public and accusations of undue severity follow, he concluded to confer with the highest authorities in relation to it. He interviewed the governor of Pennsylvania and explained the plan and its workings. The governor was convulsed with laughter and said: "Major, I heartily congratulate you on having struck the keynote and I assure you that the good people of this commonwealth will sustain you in this 'war measure.' I promise you the backing of the National Guard, if necessary, in your poetical plan of spanking reformation into your rebellious subjects."

He then called upon the chairman of the State Board of Charities, an old-time Quaker, and explained the situation to him. The Quaker smiled broadly and said: "Major, thee deserves thanks and should go on with thy noble work. It reminds me of my sainted mother, who has been in Heaven many a year. It was her favorite method of correction and I tell thee, Major, she did it well. It is proper and humane, and I approve of thee handsomely spanking thy boys into submission and obedience."

The major returned to his reformatory thoroughly convinced that his improved process of punishment would receive general approbation. The weekly spanking school became a feature of the institution, and the major's strong right arm wielded the avenging leather. The result was quite beneficial, and the infraction of the rules was less frequent and flagrant, as the inmates had a wholesome dread of the shame, disgrace and stinging pain of the major's orthodox spanks.

Pleading for Condemned Men

Attorney C.F. Mansfield of Monticello spent nearly the entire day of March 2, 1891, with Governor Joseph W. Fifer, interceding on behalf of Albert Dunham and Calvin Holden, who were condemned to hang the next Friday for the murder of Harley Russell. New evidence had come to light through the confessions of Anna Holden and Ed Holden, who were now in the Joliet penitentiary for participation in the murder.

As a result of that investigation, twenty members of the grand jury signed a statement saying they believed that Mrs. Holden had been an accomplice while Ed Holden had fired the fatal shot. A letter strongly urged the governor to wipe out the sentence of death passed upon Dunham and Holden, saying the evidence now before them did not justify any such punishment.

Gets the Reward

On June 19, 1891, Chief of Police Doyle of LaSalle identified an escaped convict from Joliet. John Kaiser, the man who had escaped from the state prison at Joliet by scaling the wall, turned up in the guise of a tramp in Sheriff Taylor's bastille. He was arrested in La Salle on Sunday night by Officer McGuire, who pulled him out of a cellar where he was in hiding.

Just after Kaiser had been taken to jail, Chief Doyle received a description and photograph of Kaiser and at once saw a startling resemblance between the man arrested and the escaped convict. As a reward of fifty dollars was offered for the capture, Doyle lost no time in coming to Ottawa. Confronted with photographs and his description, the prisoner acknowledged himself to be Kaiser and signified his willingness to return to Joliet. In scaling the prison wall on Saturday night, Kaiser sprained his ankle quite severely and cut a deep gash on the thumb of his left hand. He had stolen his civilian clothing at a farmhouse and made his way to LaSalle partially on foot and partially by riding freight trains.

ARRESTED ON HIS WAY OUT THE DOOR

James Finley Hoke, a former cashier of the Merchants' National Bank of Peoria, robbed the bank of $182,000 and escaped to Canada. He was captured and sent to the penitentiary for five years, of which he had served three years and four months. Hoke served as bookkeeper for the prison and by good behavior gained one year and eight months. On August 15, 1891, he was released from the penitentiary. As he was leaving the front door of the prison, having bidden the officers goodbye, he was met by Deputy Sheriff Thomas P. Houghton of Joliet, who arrested him on the charge of embezzlement. He was taken to Peoria on the midnight train on the Rock Island Railroad. Hoke wept bitterly and complained of persecution. As he had nineteen more indictments to answer, the chances of his spending the remainder of his life behind bars was good. Surprisingly, he was released from the prison in January 1892 but was said to be again devastated when he found that his wife had begun divorce proceedings. Friends told a reporter that they were fearful that his sense of reason would become unhinged.

J. Finley Hoke suffered many disappointments but was out of jail in less than five years due to a technicality. LeRoy (KS) Reporter, *February 12, 1887.*

A WAYWARD SON

An article of August 16, 1891, quoted a Chicago man visiting St. Louis: "I witnessed a most touching and dramatic incident the other day."

> *It was at the Union depot. Among the passengers leaving the train just in from the south was a distinguished looking old gentleman. Clinging to his arm was one of the most beautiful girls I ever saw in my whole life.*
>
> *To take the Joliet train there came down the stone steps a burly officer in citizens' clothes, and by his side was the once society favorite, George Lipe, convicted of forging his mother's name to valuable documents, who in spite of all influence brought to bear, must serve his term in the penitentiary. A steel band was about the officer's wrist. The two couples I have described met directly in front of the big gates. "Oh,*

papa," exclaimed the girl, as her face lighted up with pleasure, "here is George come to meet us after our long journey."

She rushed forward to meet the convict and impetuously grabbed both his hands. The shock the sight of the manacles produced was positively frightful. Her great eyes opened, her face blanched, she tried to speak, but could not, and then she fell fainting into the arms of her father, who bore her to a carriage. "The convict during this ordeal was a pitiable looking object. He uttered no word, but as he passed through the gate, I saw his lower lip was covered with blood. He had bitten through it. The girl, I learned was the felon's fiancée who had been in Mexico all winter."

TORMENTED

On August 21, 1891, a coroner's jury found that Christiana W. Riener killed herself with a pistol shot while insane. She was fifty-six years old and was tormented by the delusion that someone was striving to put her husband in the state's prison at Joliet and then carry her away.

PHYSICIAN BANK ROBBERS

On November 22, 1891, the people of Gardner, in Grundy County, Illinois, were torn up over a daring burglary attempted there by two local physicians. For some time, petty burglaries had been committed in the town, and several citizens had suffered losses ranging from $1 to $600. Detectives were put on the track, and on the night of November 21, they surprised Dr. McAdams and Dr. Bowes in the act of robbing the Gardner National Bank. The two physicians were assisted by a well-known liveryman, James Briggs, whose reputation in the community had been above reproach.

The physicians had been spotted for some time and were followed by a detective, who saw them effect an entrance into the bank. Just as they succeeded in blowing open the safe, he pounced on them. The burglars resisted and fired on the officers, who fired in return. Dr. McAdams was severely wounded in the neck. Both physicians were captured after a desperate struggle, but the liveryman escaped and was not heard of again. It was rumored that he was assisting the detectives, which accounts for his early flight.

McAdams had always been considered a good physician and enjoyed a fair practice. Bowes was a recent arrival, and there was some question about

The lawn and cistern were carefully tended. *Courtesy Will County Historical Museum and Research Center.*

his being a doctor, it being rumored that he was a professional burglar living under an assumed name for the purposes of which the two men were caught.

WARDEN ROBERT L. ALLEN

Robert L. Allen, the new warden of the Joliet penitentiary, was appointed postmaster of Joliet by President Grover Cleveland and held the position until his successor was appointed by President Benjamin Harrison. Allen then went into business for himself. Allen was manager of the electric light and power plant company at Joliet, with which he had been connected since its incorporation. He was a prominent man in Joliet, having lived there many years and having filled numerous positions of honor and trust. He was well acquainted with machinery and electrical appliances. Joliet City had one of the finest electrical plants in the country, and Allen was its superintendent.

THE WOMEN OF JOLIET

An article in the *St. Louis Globe-Democrat* of September 10, 1893, reported the following:

The female department of the famous Illinois Penitentiary at Joliet is up four flights of iron stairs and beyond a heavy iron-bolted door that leads to the top or fifth story of the central building. As you enter the broad hallway—airy and spotlessly neat—you are confronted by a kindly faced lady who is matron in charge—Miss Ria Madden—who has held the position for many years past. The white scrubbed floors are covered with woven rag mats of various colors and designs—the handiwork of some prisoner. At the right opens a large well-lighted room, in which there are many windows. From them a splendid view is obtained of the well-kept grounds and more distant trees. This is the main work room, where the inmates are kept at work all day long, at sewing and patching up the garments worn by the men convicts. It is terribly monotonous work—a weary, penitential task. The women sit facing the windows—their chairs in an even row. Out among the far-off trees there are glimpses of many white cottages, the happy homes of the women of Joliet. The prisoners keep their eyes bent on their work, and if the scene through the windows reminds them of the freedom they have lost, they do not show it in their repressed and hardened faces. On Sunday morning, this work room is fixed up as a chapel. Twice a month the prison chaplain conducts services. A priest takes charge one Sunday, and the other Sabbath some benevolent ladies hold services. Opposite the work room is the laundry where washing is done every day. The tubs are placed against the windows, and the women that rub and scrub Warden Allen's table linen and their own dresses upon the crinkly washboards have the same sights to beguile them that spread out before the women who darn and patch.

Next to the laundry is the dining room where Mollie Mott is employed. Between meals, she is wearing down her eight years' sentence—sprinkling clothes upon the tables and superintending the other laundresses in the adjoining room. In her prison garb Mollie is a trim-looking person. Her downcast eyes give her a very meek appearance and expression. There is nothing that indicate that she was once considered the wickedest woman in Chicago. Mollie came from a bad family—she was a "slugger," as tough as a woman can be. She married Burt Taylor, a noted cracksman. He and a gang of burglars attempted to break into a large downtown store. Detective Crowe shot and killed Burt Taylor—making Mollie Mott a burglar's widow at the age of 18. She next married Pete O'Brien, a sand bagger. While he held up unsuspecting pedestrians, Mollie would go through them with neatness and dispatch. During her second term at

The women do their sewing quietly in front of the windows. Talking was not allowed. *Courtesy Joliet Area Historical Museum, Illinois.*

Joliet, Pete O'Brien took up with another woman. Mollie swore vengeance against him, and upon her release from prison attempted to kill him.

It wasn't long before Mollie found another partner—one worthy of her nerve. Dyer Scanian was a notorious burglar and desperado—one of the toughest citizens that Chicago has yet produced. In a desperate fight with Police Officer Nolan, Scanian and Mollie nearly killed the officer. They were captured and sent to Joliet—Dyer for a ten and Mollie for an eight-year term. When she was received for her third term, Mollie seemed utterly unconcerned. Smiling at the matron, she said "I don't see why they gave Dyer more than they gave me. But the time will roll round rapidly; we are young yet and will be out before we know it."

The women prisoners sleep in dormitories. There are eight or ten cots in each room. The beds are immaculate. A prison is not provided with all the toilet preparations the women most like. Yet feminine ingenuity could supply them reasonably well. One woman, whose hair was always well dressed and shone with the luster of the finest oils, was a complete mystery to the other prisoners until she revealed the fact that she skimmed the fat from her bowl of soup. Letting it cool, she applied it to her tresses. Another woman was no less a mystery to the matron for her rosy cheeks, which unmistakably showed the presence of rouge. It was discovered that this glow of youth was imparted by the coloring matter which she obtained by chewing bits of bright red yard.

The women's prison gowns were made of blue and white gingham—of a pattern popular for kitchen aprons. Each woman had three dresses, with one saved for Sunday wear. When a white apron and a necktie were added, the chapel costume was complete. Bustles were debarred from prison wear. Corsets were, however, allowed to those who desired to preserve a small waist beneath the baggy outlines of their gingham dresses. The coiffure of the woman convict was exceedingly simple. The hair is brushed straight back and confined in a small knot at the back of the head. No bangs, frizzes or switches were allowed. The prisoners were described as a respectable looking set of women. Many of them were wrecks and in ill health when received at the prison. Some were alcoholics or opium addicts. To such, prison confinement had a most salutary effect after the first struggle was over.

At a sewing machine, hemming sheets sat Mary Anderson, alias Miller, one of the most noted shoplifters in America, serving her second term. At the time of her arrest, more than $5,000 worth of property was found in her rooms. Among the property recovered by the police was a valuable silk dress belonging to Mrs. Marshall Field. The dress had been imported from Paris and was of a peculiar pattern. It had been stolen eleven months before from the dressmaking department of Marshall Field's store. When following her chosen profession, Mary always dresses in deep mourning, with a black bonnet trimmed with crepe.

Her partner in crime was Bertha Kleinsmith, alias "Black Lena," and together they had visited nearly every large city. "Black Lena" has a record as a shoplifter that could not be equaled. "Black Lena" is known in New York and Boston, where she operated extensively. Her partner in those days was the noted Mary Scanian, alias "Kid Glove Rosy"—another famous "hoister." They were arrested in New York and served four years on Blackwell's Island. When she was released "Black Lena" traveled from city to city, stealing whatever she could lay her hands on—anything from a bolt of silk to a pair of rubber boots. She has stated herself that during a period of five years she stole from dry goods stores over $25,000 worth of silk and dress goods. In 1886 she was arrested at Chicago and sentenced for a year, and again on her release she went down for two years. She is a middle-aged woman who dresses well and is very proud of her exploits as a thief. She said she made a business of shoplifting; that was the only occupation she had ever had. She added: "But I don't steal little things. I *walk off with a bolt of silk whenever I need a new dress or want to raise money on which to have a good time, that's all."*

The severity of prison discipline for the women is not to be compared with that which Warden Allen prescribes for men. He is noted for his chivalrous treatment of the weaker sex. The women are not confined in cells, they are not given hard work, and they are under the care of a matron who treats them kindly. They are not fed on the same diet as the men. Their fare is wholesome and varied and they have dessert and tea every day. The matron's apartments are separated from the rest of the lofty prison flat by a heavy iron grating, so that at night she is securely protected against any danger from revengeful convicts.

The conduct of the women in prison by no means corresponds with the crimes for which they have been sentenced. Those who have been sent up for life, for murder, are invariably the quietest and best-behaved prisoners. On the other hand, women who have been sentenced for comparatively trifling crimes are among the worst behaved. They are oftenest in the punishment cells and cause unending worry to the prison matron and officials.

There were many African American women confined in the women's quarters at Joliet. Formerly denizens of the levee district in Chicago. Emma Ford was a stalwart-looking girl of mixed race who was employed in the laundry as head washerwoman. She was formerly a terror along Custom House place. Pearl Smith and Flossie Moore are two more of the same sort whose stomping ground was along Dearborn street near the Polk street depot. They were the robbers that waylaid so many strangers in the winter of 1892 while the victims were on their way to or from the depot. It was their practice to conceal themselves in some dark hallway, and when a man came by alone and had the appearance of having money or valuables in his possession, Flossie Moore would come dancing along the sidewalk and snatch the hat from the man's head and then dart into the hallway with it, laughing heartily as it was a great joke upon the stranger. Nine times out of ten, the unsuspecting victim would follow the woman into the hallway to regain possession of his hat. No sooner would he step into the hallway than the strong arm of Pearl Smith would shoot out of the darkness and encircle his neck, and he would meet with an embrace that would take his breath away. In the meantime, Flossie Moore would go through his pockets, and in an instant the robbers would be in possession of his money and valuables. They would then dash along the dark hall and effect their escape from a side door, while the confused victim was left to grope his way back to the street.

Among other noted women who have worn out key metal at Joliet, or who are still serving time, will be remembered such famous persons as Mollie Trussell; Theresa Sturla, alias Madeline Stiles, who killed Charley Stiles at the Palmer House; Mina Look, who received a life sentence for killing her husband at Kankakee; Josie Gurley, the abductor of little Annie Redmond; Jennie Crawe, alias "The Pock-Marked Woman," one of the cleverest house thieves that ever operated in Chicago; Dora Donegan, who at the present time is one of the worst of the women thieves who prey upon visitors to the World's Fair. Only last week, she was arrested, with Minnie May and Jennie Monroe, for holding up Marcus Kierulf at the Congress street station and relieving him of $200. Kierulf was a minister from Hamburg, Germany.

One of the worst crimes for which a woman was ever sent to Joliet was that committed by Lena Schreiner at Chicago several years ago. Finding her husband lying unconscious from drink in an alleyway between their house and the one adjoining, the woman slipped downstairs at midnight and poured a gallon of kerosene oil over him, struck a match, threw it at him and fled upstairs. In an instant Schreiner was enveloped in flames, and with a scream of agony he jumped up and ran down the street until he finally fell exhausted and dying, every particle of clothing burned from his body. The murderess was arrested, but for some time denied her guilt. Finally, however, she broke down and made a full confession. She had committed the deed because her husband had beaten her cruelly. She was let off with a ten-year term in prison.

PENITENTIARY INVESTIGATION

On March 17, 1893, the *Chicago Inter Ocean* reported on an ongoing investigation at the Joliet penitentiary. The article, "Second Day's Farce,"

Visitors pose by the lily pond. *Courtesy Joliet Area Historical Museum, Illinois.*

said that the penitentiary investigation was a disappointment so far as proving anything against Major McClaughry was concerned. One witness was said to have an avowed grudge against the major, having thrice been an unsuccessful applicant for a position in the prison. Issues of the investigation included the letting of contracts, the buying of horses for the prison farm and the use of prisoners to work on McClaughry's own home in Joliet. One witness in particular admitted a personal grudge against the warden. It was thought that the investigation might be dropped because there was not enough in the charges to go on with it any further.

McClaughry Honored

On August 1, 1893, Governor Altgeld appointed Major McClaughry general superintendent of the Illinois State Reformatory at Pontiac. President Grover Cleveland commissioned McClaughry to represent the United States at the International Prison Congress held in Paris in 1895. He received many honors and courtesies from government and prison officials. It may be recalled that McClaughry introduced the Bertillon method of identifying criminals into the United States.

Joseph Campbell

Joseph Campbell was on trial on January 22, 1894, for the murder of John Cormack. The two men had become involved in a quarrel over a game of billiards. During its progress, Campbell became incensed at a remark made by Cormack and drew a revolver. Cormack, it is said, crawled under the billiards table. While there, Campbell, it is said, shot him in the stomach, his wound resulting in fatality the next day.

A Big State Shop

On March 11, 1894, the *Chicago Sunday Tribune* featured an article on the state's manufacturing business inside the prison. The work was done by convicts under the supervision of men of experience in the various industries, and the output was sold over all America. Nothing went into Illinois markets, and the factory did not interfere with the product of local labor. It was an experiment, made absolutely necessary by the law of Illinois, which expressly forbade the contracting to private individuals of prison labor. Prison authorities throughout the country watched eagerly the result of the Joliet project. The prison had been visited by the wardens and commissioners of the penitentiaries of many states. Some of them spent days in Joliet watching with eagerness the workings of the state's manufacturing plant.

Some years earlier, the people of the state endorsed a constitutional amendment prohibiting the contract system then in vogue. The labor convicts were and had for years been contracted at a certain wage per diem. The revenue derived was quite enough to operate the prison. The contract doctrine had been followed for many years. Once before, the state had made and sold goods at the prison, but the conditions were vastly different. Farmers brought supplies to the prison and sold them, receiving boots and shoes, harnesses and other items in return. This was ruinous for local markets, and the contract system was adopted in its stead.

Governor Altgeld suggested working the convicts on state account in such industries as would least come into competition with home industries. The matter was made the subject of a special message to the legislature. Appropriations were made in accordance with Altgeld's suggestions. Occupations had to be found for the convicts as the contracts expired, power

Convicts work in the granite shop under the watchful gaze of the keeper. *Courtesy Will County Historical Museum and Research Center.*

Convicts line up to leave the stone shop. *Courtesy Will County Historical Museum and Research Center.*

plants had to be erected, machinery needed to be procured and supplies had to be purchased. In addition, a safe, certain market needed to be found for the product. The commissioners and the warden thought well before they took any decisive action. They spent $600 in traveling around the country investigating the most modern prisons and observing the most advanced ideas from experiments conducted by other prisons. Then they went to work.

THE ALIASES BY WHICH NOTED CRIMINALS ARE KNOWN TO PALS

All criminals find it convenient at times to travel under assumed names. The result is that police detectives must be familiar with one or more aliases for every crook in their record books. Not one criminal in five hundred gives his true name when arrested, unless he is known and sees it useless to lie. Some retain a fragment of self-respect and prefer not to disgrace the name borne by mother or sisters. Most criminals simply want to conceal all facts about themselves and to prevent officers of other cities from learning their whereabouts. Such criminals change their names more often than they do their shirts. They come from all parts—here today and five hundred miles away tomorrow. Their pictures are part of every well-regulated rogues' gallery.

"Snatch-em" was the alias of a famous Philadelphia hotel thief named George Lee, also alias William H. Berry. His pals were Aleck Stewart and Charles Woodward, alias "Diamond Charley." The latter received his sobriquet for once having swallowed a $500 diamond stud. He had stolen the gem from a traveling man in a Chicago hotel and was caught by the victim, but not before Woodward had placed the stone in his mouth. In order that it should not be used as evidence against him, he swallowed it, setting and all.

These crooks followed Max Freund, an agent of Freund & Company, a New York jewelry firm, all over the country until they found an opportunity to rob him at the Palmer House in Chicago. They took his sample case, containing diamonds and gold watches valued at $25,000. "Snatch-em" was caught in New York by Billy Pinkerton. Woodward was arrested in Chicago. Both were sent to Joliet for five years.

"Red Hyde," or "Cincinnati Red," was an expert hotel thief whose real name was Charles Hylebert. During the inauguration ceremonies in Washington, D.C., for President Harrison, Red Hyde and "Shang" Campbell greatly distinguished themselves by robbing three hotels in one day—the St. James, the American House and the Metropolitan—getting away with a lot of valuable stuff belonging to the guests. During the Chicago World's Fair, Red Hyde made his headquarters in Hyde Park and is undoubtedly responsible for some of the robberies perpetrated on guests at hotels in that district.

"Hoosier Bill," or "Stuttering Johnnie," as he was sometimes called, was a celebrated thief and confidence man well known all over the West. He was an escaped convict from Joliet.

"Jack Sheppard" was a street pirate when almost a baby. When he was but ten years old, he created a sensation by making a daring escape from the New York Tombs, cutting his way out and walking in sight of the guards to liberty. He later was an inmate in a dozen different prisons and escaped from them all except Joliet and the bastille at Cherry Hill, Philadelphia. "Fat Man Burke" was a Chicago celebrity whose real name was John Burke, a brother of Billy Burke, the famous bank sneak. "Fat Man" was over six feet tall and as thin as a shadow. As a thief, he was adept at the "buggy trick" and had worn out his share of key metal behind the bars at Joliet and other prisons.

"Father Becker," or the "Bogus Priest," as he was sometimes called, was a most remarkable criminal and confidence man. This sacrilegious swindler made a specialty of robbing clergymen. When not in prison doing penance for past crimes, he traveled from city to city with forged letters, claiming to be a Trappist monk. He was a smooth conversationalist and easily ingratiated himself into the good graces of Catholic clergymen. He had been recently released from a term at Joliet Prison.

"Little Lou," or Louisa Jordan, was the wife of "Pretty Tom" Bigelow and had a more eventful career. She was married a dozen times, among her husbands were such noted characters as Billy Derrigan; William J. Sharkey (a murderer whom she assisted in escaping from the New York Tombs); Aleck Purple; Dan Kelly, alias "Dan the Rioter"; and Barney Aaron, a pugilist. She procured a divorce in Chicago from the latter and married Bigelow, who was a noted thief. Little Lou had the lower half of her right ear cut off. She received this mark in Brazil, where she stole the jewels of a rich Spanish lady and was condemned to receive forty lashes on the bare back and have her ear clipped. She wore her hair combed down over the ears to hide this mark of infamy.

Boys, we must get ready to go down the road pretty soon. I guess they won't let us stay here much longer. I could see it in their eyes, they want us at Joliet and to Joliet we must go.
—Convict Dan Coughlin, 1896

The Despised Stripes

On the occasion of the Fourth of July in 1896, the convicts in Joliet first laid aside their stripes. It had been decided that inmates would wear blue or other colors as they proved themselves worthy. Each color represented an advance in obedience to the prison authorities and regulations. They were all given blue suits to start with. Changes would be made every six months, and the color of the convict's garb would show what his conduct had been.

At the hour for confining the men in their cells the night before, all wore the despised stripes. Closeted with them for the night, each man had a new and clean suit of a gray-blue color—coat, trousers and cap with a visor of leather. By 9:00 a.m. on the Fourth of July, the breakfast had been served and the convicts were dressed in their new garb. Perhaps to some, the change meant absolutely nothing, but the expressions on the faces of the others attested that they understood the alteration and the possibility that it would work. In the jail yard, the men were given permission to talk to their comrades.

The convicts assembled for chapel on Sunday. After a few songs from the convict choir, the chaplain gave a sermon. *Courtesy Joliet Area Historical Museum, Illinois.*

The yard was strung with flags, streamers and bunting. Warden Allen addressed the convicts about good behavior. He told the prisoners of the provisions of the newly enacted parole law, which went into effect July 1. He told the prisoners that the state's boarders who were not confined for murder or treason were not to be sent to the penitentiary for a specific term of years, but that the maximum and the minimum terms that applied to the offense were named and that the length of imprisonment depended on the behavior of the convict.

The prison orchestra, which occupied a portion of the platform, furnished a great variety of tunes and medleys, and the men danced. Twenty of the convicts took turns in meeting on a second platform in boxing contests and wrestling matches, and two contortionists performed. The musicians formed themselves into a choir and sang popular songs. The prisoners were led back to their cells for a dinner of roast pork and potatoes. Each man was given five cigars and a piece of square tobacco. The men were given the privilege to write to their friends.

The women participated in a cake walk in the corner of the yard; the cake was cut and eaten on the spot. They were treated to bananas, oranges, candy and popcorn. They enjoyed drink mixtures of ice cream and lemonade. They spent most of their time dancing and were put into their cells after two and a half hours.

WOMEN'S PRISON ACROSS THE ROAD

On November 16, 1896, the women were marched out of their old quarters in the main building, down the lawn and across the street to the new female prison. Many of the women had not been outside the prison walls for years and looked forward to the trip with great excitement. The officials also anticipated with pleasure the opening of the new building. All were glad to exchange the dingy rooms in which they had been living for the large and well-lighted apartments.

For several years, between sixty and seventy women had been crowded into a few small rooms on the top floor of the warden house, where the female department was located. Sanitary conditions in the rooms were bad. In the dormitories, twenty-five cots were crowded into a space originally intended for twelve or fifteen. There were no windows in the cells, which were dark and poorly ventilated. The work rooms were small. The laundry and the dining room were the same. One small room, not removed from the rest, served as a hospital. These conditions menaced the health of both the inmates and the officers and made the administration of discipline difficult.

The year before, efforts of the prison commissioners to afford relief to this department were successful. The state legislature made an appropriation for a new building, separate from the main institution, for the use of female prisoners. Work was begun on it in the spring of 1896. Convicts quarried the stone for the new structure within a few rods of the spot where its foundations were laid. All summer long, the work had been going on toward completion until, at last, the building was ready for occupation.

Outside, the new prison looked like a small copy of the larger institution. The same style of architecture was used for its limestone exterior. Round turrets at the corners suggested a medieval castle. Two lofty towers guarded the front entrance. A stone wall would replace the high board fence that surrounded the building, making the resemblance even more striking.

The large hall upon which the front doorway opened also served as a reception room. At the left were special apartments for the matron; on the right were rooms for the transaction of routine business. Beyond these were the rooms in which the convicts spent their working hours and the chapel. The last was a much-needed innovation. Hitherto there had been no place but the knitting shop, half-filled with machinery, where the women

A drawing of the new women's penitentiary that opened in 1896. It was said to be the finest in the world. Chicago Tribune, *November 15, 1896.*

could be gathered for religious or other meetings, and even that could not accommodate them all at once. The new chapel was provided with chairs enough to seat all and had in addition a good organ.

Farther on were the dining room, laundry, drying room, kitchen and general workrooms. In the kitchen, a new line of work would be inaugurated for the prisoners. Formerly, the regular three meals a day were sent to the women from the main culinary department. Now, they would be cooked here, separately, by the prisoners themselves. There was also a sanitary improvement. In place of the two bathtubs, with which it took two days for all the prisoners to bathe, there were now a dozen new, white tubs of the latest pattern, fitted with proper plumbing.

But the most interesting feature of any prison is the cells. These occupied the whole of the large space above the workrooms in the long wing that ran back from the front edifice. A double row of barred windows on the outside marked the location of a double tier of cells within. There were twenty-five cells in each tier, and as the opposite wall was lined with them in the same manner, there were altogether one hundred cells. These would accommodate the prisoners separately for a long time to come. Each cell was lighted with a good-sized window; at some time in the day, either morning or afternoon, the sunlight shone into each.

Four or five large, airy rooms on the second floor of the front building were used for a hospital and a physician's laboratory. Rooms for the matron's assistants occupied the rest of the floor. Above, on the third floor, far removed from everything else, was the "solitary" prison. Here were three cells, where, though only in the most extreme cases, refractory prisoners would be handcuffed to the grate door during working hours and fed only bread and water. Throughout the building, every hall and every stairway leading from the actual prison to the rooms occupied by the administration were carefully shut off by iron gratings so that escape was practically impossible.

The enclosure within the stone wall surrounding the building would be devoted to grass and flowers. Here, the women would be allowed to come out in the open air once every day. To those whose eyes had for many years seen the sky only through iron bars, this would be a much-valued privilege.

The number of female convicts at the institution had doubled in the previous six years. It was now understood that prisons for women were a necessity. But the State of Illinois was doing much to make imprisonment a means of preventing and discouraging crime. Many a stubborn character, who, if severely punished, would have been incorrigible, entered quietly into prison life after a friendly talk with the matron. In every way, the women were encouraged to begin a respectable and useful life on their release. The regular, orderly work of prison life had a good effect in this direction. There was a wholesome atmosphere of cheerfulness among the inmates.

More seclusion was granted to the women than to the men. Their department was closed to the public. Ordinary visitors did not enter it. The number of African American women among the inmates was noticeable. "Forty out of the sixty-eight are colored," said the matron. "They come in for petty thieving, robberies, and occasionally for murder. Of all these, murderers are invariably the most trustworthy. Of course, you can easily understand that a woman in for habitual stealing, for instance, would be likely to continue her thefts here. Now, with a woman in for murder, the case is different. That offense may be the great and only one of her life. These women are almost always trusty here."

Although some of the women spent their evenings in trivial amusements, many of them read. Fiction, of course, held the most prominent place in the works selected. Mary J. Holmes was by far the most popular author. Schoolbooks were, however, much read. Crocheting was a favorite occupation with the women, and some of them had quite a collection of elaborate tidies and other pieces of fancy work.

For the inmates, every day was the same. The female prisoner rose to the sound of the gong at 6:00 a.m. She had her breakfast and at 7:00 a.m. went to work at her allotted task. The noon hour lasted from 11:40 a.m. to 1:00 p.m. Then all went to work again for the afternoon, stopping at about 5:00 p.m. The closing hour varied with the length of daylight in summer and winter. From suppertime until 8:30 p.m., the women spent their time very much as they wished, in their cells and dormitories.

One privilege they had previously enjoyed would be missed in the new building. Opportunities for talking were greatly lessened, for each woman was put into a separate cell, in place of the dormitories where many of them had slept before. At 8:30 p.m., all were locked up, lights were put out and silence was enforced. Sunday, of course, varied the workday program. Regular chapel service was held, and every fourth week, a welcome visit was paid to the women by Salvation Army members of the local post. The routine in the new building was the same.

McClaughry Resumes Duties

On March 1, 1897, Governor John Riley Tanner requested that McClaughry resume the duties of warden of the State Penitentiary at Joliet. Major McClaughry was at that time sixty-two years old. It was said that few penitentiary wardens in the country knew as much of penology as did the major.

Editor Dunlop's Sentence

On March 24, 1897, Joseph R. Dunlop, proprietor and editor of the *Chicago Dispatch*, commenced his two-year sentence in Joliet. After a desperate legal battle of two years, he was compelled to go to prison. Dunlop's fight against the sentence was no doubt largely actuated by the fear that his imprisonment would be made unusually severe in return for the *Dispatch*'s vicious fight with the police department four years earlier, when Warden McClaughry was chief of police in Chicago. The numerous statements from his physicians regarding his impaired health were referred to Dr. Ferguson, the prison physician, who, after a careful examination of Dunlop, advised the warden as to his physical qualifications for prison labor. The most that Dunlop could hope for was only such treatment as the common convict received.

6

ADOLPH LUETGERT

"The Sausage Vat Murderer"

Adolph Louis Luetgert had come to America in the 1870s and settled in the Windy City, where there was a large German population. He had tried farming and tanning but eventually made it big with his spiced meat products and became known as the "Sausage King." Chicagoans knew him as the best maker of German sausages in the city. His first wife died and left him with a son, Arnold. In the 1880s, Luetgert married Louisa Bicknesse, a small, fragile woman who was ten years younger. The couple would soon have two sons, Elmer and Louis. The family lived in comfortable fashion near the sausage factory, on the corner of Hermitage and Diversey Parkway in Chicago.

On the evening of May 1, 1897, Louisa disappeared. When neighbors asked Luetgert, he shrugged his shoulders, saying his wife had left him but that she would probably be back before long. They had a quarrel, he explained, and she had gone off in a huff. The missing woman's brother reported her disappearance to the police. The investigation turned up evidence of infidelity, financial bankruptcy and threats against the missing woman. The evidence of witnesses led police to the factory. In the middle vat were found two gold rings, one bearing the initials "L.L.," the other being a small guard ring. Flakes of bones and a tooth were discovered, as well as a skull among some animal bones in the yard. The detective took these to an anthropologist at the Field Columbian Museum, who identified them as being those of a human female.

An ad for Luetgert Sausage, Chicago's finest. Unfortunately, the news spoiled people's appetites. *Bizzarepedia.*

Luetgert was accused of luring his wife into the factory and slitting her throat. He had then dismembered the body with a cleaver. The watchman was asked to bring down barrels of caustic potash. Leutgert had later removed the skull and other large bones from the boiling mass, throwing them in the yard among the pile of animal bones. The next day, when he came back to finish cleaning up, he found the sheriff's deputies there to keep the factory closed during bankruptcy proceedings.

When the story hit the newspapers, the entire populace of Chicago experienced great difficulty at mealtimes. Even when chemists and medics at Rush Medical College found it would have been almost impossible for Luetguert to have made away with his wife in this manner, the ban on sausage was not lifted. In those days, free lunches in the saloons flourished, but even the barrelhouse bums refused a free hot dog. Manufacturers of sausage were almost driven out of business.

The prosecution obtained a corpse and placed it in the factory vat, boiling it in caustic potash for two hours. They reported that the fleshy parts of the body were gone, as were all the bones except the larger ones. Luetgert's lawyer claimed that he had also done a test using a corpse and that the boiling process did not dissolve the corpse. The defense maintained that Mrs. Luetgert was not dead and that no crime had been committed. A "Mrs. Luetgert" was found in every city. Adolph Luetgert was found guilty and sentenced to Joliet State Prison for life.

He arrived at Joliet in March 1898. It was said that he was a model prisoner. He maintained a confidence in his chances for a rehearing of the case. In the spring of 1899, he began working in the cold-storage plant at the prison. He had a lot of experience and made a valuable contribution there. J.D. Leland, purchasing agent who supervised Luetgert, said: "He was one of the best men I ever had in the meat shop. He was reliable and trustworthy. He liked to work." But one day in mid-July, Luetgert rejected some of the meat that came in on a delivery. The Armour & Company

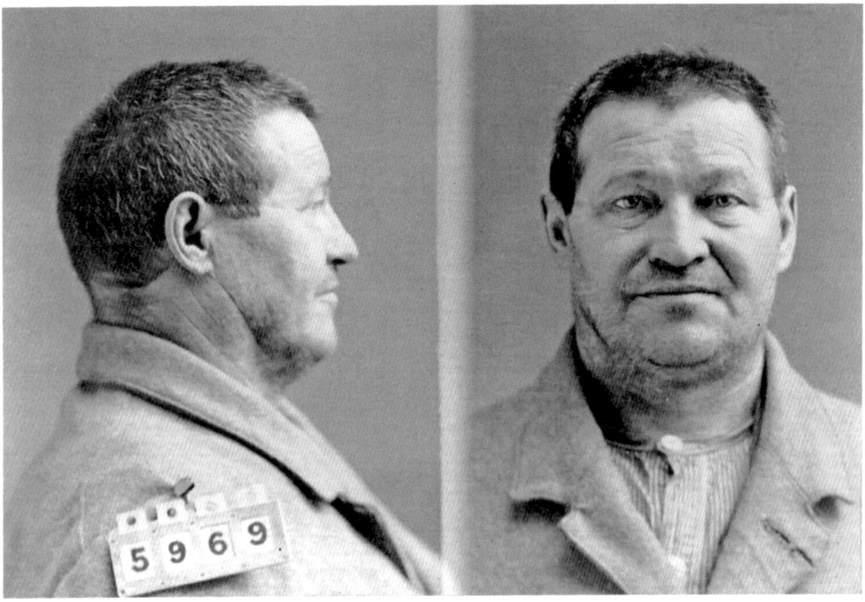

Adolph Luetgert's mug shot. *Courtesy Illinois State Archives.*

agent came up to find out what the trouble was, and the disagreement became heated. Luetgert ended up being sent to solitary for a couple of hours.

On July 27, 1899, Adolph Luetgert marched with the others to breakfast and returned with the meal in his pail. A few minutes later, a keeper heard groans coming from the cell and ran to the door. Luetgert was writhing on his cot as if in great agony. By the time the prison doctor got to him, he was dead of a heart attack. Louisa supposedly haunted him during his incarceration in Joliet Prison until the day he died. On May 1, the anniversary of Louisa's death, it was said that she can still be seen roaming her old stomping grounds.

7

JOLIET PRISON IN THE NEWS, *1897-1903*

Prison Guard Owns to Theft

On July 20, 1898, Elmer A. Lutes, farm guard at the prison, confessed to the larceny of tallow from the state valued at $400. He also acknowledged having been an accomplice of Frank Popp, an ex-convict, in pilfering several hundred dollars' worth of rattan furniture from the prison warehouse used by the Joliet Rattan and Reed Company. The day before, Popp had confessed to the Chicago police, implicating Lutes in the theft. Warden McClaughry and Deputy Warden Luke began an investigation. Lutes was brought before them and was unable to withstand the searching examination to which he was subjected. After about an hour's weak attempt to maintain ignorance of the charges, he broke down and made a full confession. Lutes lived on the prison farm in the little home furnished by the state. His duties as farm guard made him a sort of overseer of certain work. He began a systematic robbery of the state two years earlier during the last year of ex-warden Allen's administration. He then superintended soapmaking.

The state furnished two barrels of tallow for use in making soap. Lutes made up one barrel and left one loaded in the big wagon. The tallow was secreted in a little room partitioned off in the barn, which Lutes always kept locked. It was later sold to an old man in Joliet who gathered up bones. Lutes confessed that his operations in the tallow line in the previous two or more years had netted him over $400. This was in addition to his dealings with Popp in pilfering the furniture. Popp had driven from Chicago at night to pick up the stolen furniture and divide the proceeds.

Tuberculosis, the Penitentiary Scourge

In May 1899, it was shown that tuberculosis was the scourge of the state penitentiaries in the United States. In some of the penal institutions, the annual death rate from tubercular diseases was as low as 2.04 in every 1,000 convicts. In the Illinois Penitentiary at Joliet, the annual rate at which inmates died from tuberculosis was 16.3 in every 1,000. In ten years, 223 inmates of Joliet died of tuberculosis. The greater meaning of these statistics is discovered when taken in connection with the fact that most of the inmates of state prisons were under thirty-five years of age and the average length of the prison term about two years.

Just Pay the Bill

Sam Rightsell refused to pay his bill to a doctor in Fairbury, Illinois. The doctor went to the county courthouse in Pontiac and got a judgment against Sam. The Fairbury constable was instructed to take and sell enough of Sam's livestock to pay the bill and give the money to the doctor. Constable Joseph Galloway went to Rightsell's house when he was not home and removed the animals. When Rightsell got home and realized what had happened, he went to several stores and bought hundreds of rounds of ammunition. He found Galloway walking with his five-year-old daughter. He fired twice, but the gun malfunctioned. Galloway shot Rightsell in the hip, but he got away. Rightsell hid in the basement of a nearby house. The owners called the police, and City Marshal Fred Baird was dispatched to the house. Baird started down the stairs, and Rightsell shot him dead. Rightsell died in Joliet Prison.*

Warden McClaughry Promoted

On July 1, 1899, at the personal solicitation of President William McKinley, Warden McClaughry accepted the appointment of warden of the U.S. Penitentiary at Leavenworth, Kansas. He began the work of building the great federal prison. He served as warden of Leavenworth for six years.

* From Dale C. Maley, *History of Murders Committed in Fairbury, Illinois* (N.p.: Artephius Publishing, 2020).

Visitors pose on the lawn by the cistern. *Courtesy Will County Historical Museum and Research Center.*

Known as the "humane warden," McClaughry required his subordinates to strictly adhere to his motto during his administration: "Treat a prisoner as if he was a man—make a man of him."

DESPERATE DEEDS DEMAND DESPERATE MEANS

The Joliet Prison authorities received notice on September 30, 1899, of the arrest in California of the notorious convict and jailbreaker Brank Steadman, alias "Wheeler," alias "Ohio Fatty." His criminal record was known to the police of most large cities. He had affected two escapes from the San Quentin, California prison, and once from Joliet, and also had the distinction of having stabbed his cellmate to death while an inmate of the Folsom prison.

In 1893, he was sentenced to a seven-year term in Joliet. In May 1894, his keeper took him to the engine house to do some work. The keeper had stepped into a small tool room to get something, and Steadman slammed the door shut and fastened it with a hook, imprisoning the unwary officer. He ran to the west wall, forty feet in height, which he scaled by means of a rope ladder. The guard who was locked in the tool house raised such a howl that the prison was soon aroused, and in a few minutes, the walls were surrounded. But it was soon discovered that the bird had flown, the rope ladder pointing the way.

A year later, he was arrested for a burglary at San Francisco and sent up to San Quentin. There, he was put to work with other convicts in the machine shop. He noticed that every evening at the time the men working in the shop were lined up to be marched away, the machinery was stopped. The window leading to an adjacent roof was not far from the top of the big driving belt of the engine. From that roof it was possible to reach the outer wall of the prison. Beyond the wall was freedom.

He thought that the big belt might be the means of carrying him to liberty. He learned by constant observation just how many times the belt went around after the engine shut down. One evening, as the wheel began to lose its momentum, he sprang from the line, leaped to the belt with outstretched arms and grappled both edges of the broad leather. Outward and upward he swung until he reached the topmost point of the circumference. The nicety of his calculations had reaped its reward. He sprang through the window and was gone before anyone had recovered their astonishment.

MAUD BALLINGTON BOOTH (1865–1948)

I will help you over the rough places, but I will not carry you.

Maud Ballington Booth was a Salvation Army leader, advocate for prisoners and their families and cofounder of the Volunteers of America. In 1895, the warden of San Quentin Prison invited her to speak before the prisoners in the chapel. Booth went, prepared with an evangelistic address. She had never visited a state prison before, and the vivid, lasting impression she received was that of a hopelessness beyond Dante's Inferno. Filled with this, she spoke so feelingly that when she called on those who desired to lead a better life, even in prison, more than two hundred men rose, many of them blinded with tears. Going back to New York, Booth went to Sing Sing, having no plans laid out and no theories in reserve. With only tender sympathy and love, she began to seek the individual in each prison, until "my boys," as she called them, were her boys for life. Thousands of them, even when back to honorable stations in life, wrote to her—some of them as they had never wrote to their mother.

The first Hope Hall was established in a large dwelling house in Harlem, New York. It had wide, pleasant grounds, and a five-year lease was taken. Funds especially solicited furnished it as a simple, cheerful home. Then, when news of the establishment got out, residents of Harlem rose in wrath, not wanting ex-convicts living among them. Firmly and kindly, Booth stood by her work. Next door to her was a well-known sculptor who was especially distressed. When Hope Hall was moved into a new, $12,000 home at Flushing, Long Island, this sculptor went to Booth expressing regret at her going and fear that he "might not get such good neighbors again." The

Maud Ballington Booth founded Hope House to help convicts transition to life on the outside. *Volunteers of America.*

second Hope Hall was in Chicago, and it was said that the neighbors often did not even realize its mission.

"Look up and hope" was the motto on the little blue-and-white button that each member of the league wore in ten prisons across the United States. Prisons had an inflexible rule that when a visitor, official or guard passes a prisoner, he look at the ground. "Think of this," she says, "you who may have found fault with the ex-convict who could not 'look you in the face.' Think of the years of degradation in the lock step and see if you can criticize the loose, shuffling movement of the feet which anywhere catches the eye of a city detective and marks the man as an ex-convict. Think what it is, when years and years of such discipline have crushed out almost human semblance in the man, to ask of him that he come out into the glaring day, look every man in the face and prepare to take up the honorable work of the world, which will not let him touch the hem of its garments." Hope Hall was the haven, the breathing place, the halfway house where such men could nerve themselves and be nerved for the struggle.

On January 28, 1900, Maud Ballington Booth, frail in health, speaking before an assemblage in the parlors of Mrs. L.A. Coonley Ward, received from those present $900 for the cause of released convicts from Joliet Prison. She made a simple plea for "the man who never had a chance," for the wrongdoer who had no hope of escape from the story of his wrongdoing, and she told the story of how Hope Hall in Chicago within fifteen months had turned 161 ex-convicts back into the world, where they were proving themselves worthy of another chance at life. "I do not want to die and leave my boys in prison until the work for their salvation is on a more solid foundation," she said. Hope Hall needed $3,000 a year to run at its present limited capacity. The public was asked to come forward and help, as Booth had a serious heart malady and shouldn't "be left to waste her strength and shorten her life in getting the means with which to prosecute her work."

Warden E.J. Murphy wrote in a *Chicago Tribune* article that Booth's visits to Joliet were always anticipated by the prisoners, even more than Christmas or the Fourth of July, and that her meetings were the most unique and interesting services held in the prison chapel. "She is known as the 'Little Mother,' who has consecrated her life to work among criminals and outcasts. When she goes to Joliet, the chapel always is filled. While their attendance at church services is purely optional with the prisoners, they all eagerly embrace the opportunity whenever the 'Little Mother' comes to talk to them and bid them look up and hope."

MARCUS TRAIN ROBBERS

On the night of August 5, 1902, five men robbed a train on the Burlington Railroad. They stopped the train with a red-light signal and put the engineer and fireman under guard. They blew open the safe with nitroglycerine and rifled the contents. They uncoupled the engine from the express car and attempted to make their escape. One of the men was accidentally shot when his companion's gun discharged. Believing him to be mortally wounded, they killed him and threw his body from the engine. They abandoned the engine, letting it run on until it stopped beyond Hanover. The men escaped in a skiff at Apple River. The dead man was later identified, and two of the robbers were caught. While they were in the Carroll County Jail, the prisoners made several desperate attempts to escape, but their efforts were thwarted by the sheriff. They were convicted of highway robbery with deadly weapons and sentenced to the state penitentiary for life.

JOHN HOLLER AND HIS MULE

John Holler was sentenced to the Wisconsin state prison. The decrepit old burglar was at that time serving time at the Illinois prison at Joliet. Colonel Clarkson, who was head probation officer of the prison, was in Kenosha in October 1915 and discussed Holler's case with Judge Randall. "You hit us below the belt when you sentenced John Holler in Wisconsin," the colonel said. "He was just about the most useful prisoner we had at Joliet prison. For years he had been driving the mule which was used in collecting scrap paper about the prison. He had driven that old mule for years and since Holler came over into Wisconsin to work, the mule has absolutely refused to be comforted. We have either got to get Holler back to Joliet or get a new mule and I guess the latter course would be the cheaper."

Johnny and his mule. *Courtesy Joliet Area Historical Museum, Illinois.*

FOURTH OF JULY

There is only one day in the year, for it to draw near I sigh
It's the greatest day of any—the fourth day of July.
I long for the big dinner, lemonade and cigars
That the state supplies to her "patriots" behind bars.
When the day arrives each year to respect the Declaration
The Warden turns us all loose in the yard for recreation.
We enjoy ourselves like school children, and as the hours go by
We bless the men who signed that sheet on the fourth day of July.
—Inmate, Joliet Penitentiary, 1902

8

FAINTING BERTHA

Bertha Liebecke was in and out of asylums and institutions from a young age. She gained notoriety by extracting nickels from streetcar conductors' pockets and later appealing to judicial sympathy by fainting in the bailiff's arms. She would go into jewelry stores and ask to see expensive rings. When the jeweler's back was turned, she substituted a cheap ring she'd brought with her for one of the expensive ones in the tray. Arrested, she was often able to charm her way out of it, saying she'd never get into trouble again. She shoplifted constantly, taking anything that appealed. If suspected, she would faint.

The police named her "Fainting Bertha." She was examined by the insanity board and begged for help. Officials went in together to buy the girl a ticket to Kansas City, where she said her sister lived. She instead went to Joplin, Missouri, entered a pawnshop and sneaked a couple of valuable diamond rings. After her arrest, one of the rings was found in her stocking and the other in her hair. When taken to jail, she begged officers to give her laudanum to end her life. The *Quad City Times* stated that "she has probably hypnotized the police" by now. It was reported that Bertha was one of the cleverest "kleptomaniacs" in the business. A story in the *Nebraska State Journal* reported: "Perhaps it would be more proper to speak of Bertha as seeking fresh streams. For Bertha fishes; she fishes for suckers. And she is the best fisherwoman that ever came around these parts."

In the spring of 1901, Bertha was incarcerated in a Missouri asylum. Five male attendants were discharged on her account. She soon escaped. She

"FAINTING BERTHA"
The Most Troublesome Prisoner in Illinois
She has been in Seven State Institutions
Escaped a dozen times and none wants her

The newspapermen delighted in the exploits of "Fainting Bertha." This banner was run by the *Chicago Tribune* on January 20, 1907. Chicago Tribune.

traveled to Omaha to see her mother and sister. Soon after arriving, she saw a man who looked like an easy mark. Bertha stood with a pensive look on her face. Her lip trembling, it was plain that she was in great trouble. Noting the worried and sympathetic glances of the stranger, Bertha burst into tears. The man offered aid. The weeping woman had just begun to tell her troubles when she fell to the floor. After she was revived, Bertha departed, apologizing and thanking the stranger. After she'd been gone for several minutes, the man realized his roll of greenbacks was missing from his vest pocket. The police realized that "Fainting Bertha" was back in town. She was arrested, and the money was found in her suitcase.

She first became an inmate of the Joliet penitentiary in February 1903 following her conviction at Galesburg on a charge of larceny. In July, she was transferred to the Illinois State Hospital for the Insane at Kankakee. There, while pretending to be in a faint, she caught the attendants off their guard and escaped.

She escaped from the workhouse and made her way to the depot. There, she met two detectives. She told them she had been pardoned by the mayor on the promise that she leave the city. But she had no money to get to Atchison, where her poor mother lived. The detectives hustled around and got the money for her and saw her safely on her train. Half an hour later, they received word from the central station that Bertha had escaped and to watch all outgoing trains for her.

Bertha made her next appearance in Kansas City in March 1904. She checked into the Midland Hotel under the name of Bertha Rose. One night, she appeared on the balcony overlooking the lobby and directed the orchestra leader to play "The Holy City." As the strains of the sacred song swept over the lobby, a woman's voice suddenly startled the guests of the hotel, and Fainting Bertha demonstrated that what she lacked as a vocalist she made up in self-possession. It was said that the song had never sounded worse than under the treatment of Bertha, who rambled through all of the verses, unmindful of the stiff smiles of the trapped listeners. As soon as a bellboy could reach the orchestra leader, the music ceased, and Bertha retired from under the limelight. As the final note died away, there was a grand rush to the bar. A day or two later, Bertha was in jail on a robbery charge. When the property clerk at police headquarters was overhauling her baggage, he found a silver card tray and a cake dish marked "Midland Hotel." She'd been singing "The Holy City" the same night she was stealing the silver.

On June 29, 1904, the Reverend Charles W. Savidge, preaching at the People's Church in Omaha, took for his subject the life and causes of the present condition of Fainting Bertha. He used for his text "Brethren, if any of you do err," from James 5:19.

"My subject is a peculiar one," said the speaker.

> *But I believe there is as good a sermon in this living example of a ruined life as there is in anything. Who is to blame for this woman's life? Herself, say you? No, there are other causes besides her own weakness. The first cause I put down to the fact that at her home and among her acquaintances drinking was quite common. The next, I think, is due to the people of Omaha and Council Bluffs, who, when she was down dragged her still further down with hooting, laughter and scorn, and last, her life of sin dates from the time of her betrayal.*
>
> *I was surprised to hear from her that the partner of her crime was not a young man, but an old man. This gray-haired, debauched devil, with his experience among women, a past master in vice, is perhaps today a respected member of some community and has probably forgotten the innocent girl whose arm he took one day and drove to hell, and finally brought her down to what she is. He may forget, but an all-seeing God knows where to put the blame.*
>
> *I will never forget the look she gave me when I visited her last week at the city jail. If you want to see the devil in a woman's face, look at her when she's in an angry mood. When she knew my errand, she softened down, and after I had spoken to her for a little time, the woman who had but a moment*

> *before given me the look of a fiend incarnate now laid her head on the table and sobbed as if her heart would break. She told me she was a respectable girl until she was 17 years old; now she is 24. In seven short years, from first being an ardent Sunday school student, she has become a criminal with such a record that three states have given her up as hopeless. Nebraska drove her to Kansas, Kansas hounded her to Iowa and Iowa turned her out. We of Council Bluffs and Omaha, who dragged her down, must now lift her up. The girl is not wholly bad. When she escaped from prison the other day and had to run like some wild animal, hiding where she could, not daring to ask help from anyone, where did she go? Back to her old mother, where she could lay her poor hunted head on her mother's breast and sob out her penitence. Poor child and poor mother!*

Mr. Savidge said that Bertha Liebecke was fond of fruit and asked that some mothers who have daughters of their own send her some while she is in the city jail, waiting the next term of court, when she would once again be tried.

On October 6, she met a man in a crowd while watching a parade and relieved him of $140. Three days later, she was in St. Louis drinking with two men. Once they were intoxicated, she fainted and relieved them of their wallets. A few days later, she was in Chicago and stole a sealskin coat valued at $360. In November 1905, Bertha was brought back to Illinois to face larceny charges. Bertha said that she preferred to die rather than return to the Kankakee insane asylum. She twice set her own clothing on fire in attempts at suicide in her jail cell. While she was badly burned, her injuries were not serious.

In February 1906, she was arrested, convicted and sentenced to Joliet Prison. Records show her to have been the most unruly prisoner ever confined in that institution, male or female. She would appear in a window that overlooked the street with her clothing torn to ribbons, shrieking that she was being murdered. She heaped unspeakable abuse upon matrons and guards alike, and no language was too foul. She slept in daylight and shrieked all night. The tortured officials at Joliet sent her to the asylum. In October, she was discharged from the hospital at Kankakee and taken to back to Joliet. Shortly after, she was taken from there to the Asylum for the Insane at Elgin. She'd become violent and was placed in the "dangerous ward." She escaped and was returned.

In December, a key disappeared, but no one suspected that Bertha had taken it. Bertha quietly slipped out again during Christmas festivities a few days later. She went to a dry-goods store at Elgin. While waiting at the train station, she saw two attendants from the asylum approaching. She screamed for the police and asked to be taken to the station for protection. While in the patrol wagon, Bertha showed the officer the garments she had stolen, telling him, "I stole all these things, but don't tell anyone." The policeman promised, and she gave him the booty. At the station, her identity was discovered. She was taken back to the institution and placed under guard.

At 27 years old, Bertha was called "the most troublesome person who ever crossed the state line from any direction at any time."

A reporter for the *Chicago Tribune* speculated: "Just how large a cash bonus the state treasury today might be willing to advance could it be assured of Bertha's deportation forever beyond the confines of Illinois is something difficult to estimate, but it is certain that in the asylums for the insane at Kankakee, Elgin, and perhaps-Bartonville, and in the state penitentiary at Joliet, there are attendants on salaries who would make personal contributions to help swell the possible fund."

Authorities were at a loss. She had escaped twice from both Elgin and Kankakee. They insisted that she was not crazy and should be locked up in Joliet, which did not want her back. When Dr. Zeller at Bartonville asked that Bertha be assigned to his institution, both Elgin and Joliet were relieved. Bertha was sent to the Bartonville Asylum on January 3, 1907. A week later, the attorney general at Springfield ruled that Bertha had been illegally detained there. He argued that, under the law, since the completion of the Asylum for the Criminally Insane at Chester, there was no other place for her. Agents of the Joliet penitentiary set out for Bartonville with instructions that Bertha be taken to Chester.

When the agents arrived, Bertha and two nurses met the officers at the station. Bertha shook hands with the matron, introduced the others and slipped out of the station to the rear platform of the car, which had just pulled up to the platform. The parole agent and penitentiary matron were left staring after her. Forty-eight hours later, she was arrested in Peoria with $1,000 worth of stolen goods on her. Dr. Zeller again argued for Bertha to stay at Bartonville. Chester had never housed a woman. "We can do more for her here than anywhere else in the state."

Bertha would gain nothing by fainting at Bartonville; a dash of cold water was promised her in this event. She couldn't secure keys by fainting, either, for there were no keys on the doors. Zeller explained that if patients fought against restraints, officials would simply take away the show of restraint. "Human vigilance is the greatest safeguard for the insane."

In April, Bertha approached the members of an investigation committee. With tears in her eyes, she begged to be allowed to go home to see her aged mother. She claimed that she was dying at Bartonville; Bertha's health was shattered. On June 13, 1908, Betha escaped from the tuberculosis tent at the Bartonville asylum. She was recaptured the next day. Bertillon records showed that Bertha had been in two hundred jails and five asylums and had served three terms in penitentiaries.

She was arrested at a hotel in Lincoln, Nebraska. In her room were items from several department stores. She was taken to the police station and confined in the woman's ward. She took a chair and smashed out the window, then broke the chair beating it against the iron bars of the cell. She was placed in a solid steel cell in the men's ward. Cursing at the officers who attempted to transfer her, she was finally picked up and carried to the cell, flailing and kicking. She was taken to the penitentiary on a three-year sentence.

At first, she was docile and enjoyed embroidering. Just as the warden started to think things were going well, Bertha started cursing and racing up and down the hallway like a maniac. She drove the other women inmates into their rooms. The warden said to lock her in her room and let her work off her frenzy. After two hours of cursing and screaming, she finally became quiet. But the fits of rage came more quickly after that. She threatened to kill all the women convicts. Three men held her to keep her from killing a female prisoner for whom Bertha had developed a special hatred. It was recommended that she be transferred to one of the state hospitals for the insane.

Bertha said she was glad to be taken away from the penitentiary and that she would give no further trouble. She was permitted to go about the grounds if accompanied by a female attendant. She would sometimes run away but would be quickly brought back, her pockets loaded down with razors, knives or keys. She objected strenuously to being searched and disliked having to give up the items.

On October 23, 1913, Bertha completed her penitentiary sentence and was released from the hospital. She declared that she would rather spend ten years in a prison than two years in that asylum. "Never again will I plead insanity." She said she had made up her mind to follow the straight and narrow path. The Reverend Charles W. Savidge took her under his reformatory wing. Bertha was brought into police headquarters screaming, cursing and fighting after being arrested, charged with being drunk. When the preacher offered to take charge of her and cure her of her criminal tendencies, she was turned over to him by the state authorities. The minister and his parishioners fasted all day, praying in the church. Twelve hours later, the reverend announced that the devils had been put to rout. Bertha was preparing for evangelistic work. In April, she was back in Kansas City, saying that she'd been converted to religion. She was selling copies of her book, *Clothed in Scarlet*, for twenty-five to fifty cents a copy and lecturing on the streets, telling about the wages of sin and her years in prison.

On May 7, the headline in Omaha, Nebraska was "Demon Rum Follows Devils; Fainting Bertha Goes to Jail." Bertha had returned to her fainting stunts and the day before was drunk. In June, officers recognized her and found five empty suitcases in her hotel room, where she was registered under an alias. While in custody, Bertha had made three attempts to leap to her death. Passing an open window, twelve feet from the ground, she dived for it. She struck a detective who stood in the way. She then started crawling toward the window, but another officer interfered. On the way downstairs, Bertha again tried one of her headlong dives. This time, a newspaper reporter was in the way. He and Bertha rolled to the bottom of the stairway. When placed in the elevator, she threw herself against the walls. She was finally lodged in a padded cell.

When arrested in Omaha in February 1915, she agreed to accept a prison sentence. Her mood soon changed, and she wanted out. She smashed everything that could be broken, captured the hose from the janitor and wet down everyone within reach, took poison, set fire to herself and almost burned down the jail. At the penitentiary, she kicked out windowpanes, threw plates and food in every direction, kicked the other prisoners, pushed them down and gave voice to the most effective line of "cuss words" ever heard in the place. When the guards put her in a room by herself, she got a handkerchief and hanged herself from the bed but was discovered in time to save her life.

Bertha was clearly not pleased when this mug shot was taken. Des Moines Register, *December 7, 1919.*

The punishments of the prison had no effect on her. "Four or five days of such action left the guards, the prison officials and the prisoners limp." But Bertha seemed to thrive on it. Guards were hit, kicked, cuffed, scratched, bitten and spat upon. At first, the other prisoners enjoyed it and incited Bertha to keep it up. But when they found that she could keep things going without their assistance, long after their desire for it had ceased, they petitioned to have her transferred.

On July 22, 1918, Bertha assaulted a nurse, throwing acid in the face of an attendant at the asylum. The formaldehyde resulted in permanent injury to the woman's eyesight. Bertha died in 1939 at the state mental hospital in Lincoln, Nebraska, where she had lived in obscurity for more than twenty years.

9

JOLIET PRISON IN THE NEWS, 1903–13

Central Dining Room

On May 30, 1903, a central dining room was opened. The inmates would no longer have to march, fill their pails and eat in their cells.

Just As the Doctors Said

On April 7, 1905, it was reported that the state board of health was investigating the health conditions at the prison in Joliet. A great many prisoners had been taken down with consumption in the previous year. They were especially at risk, as they got little sunlight and were too closely crowded together, which made for "bad air." The public was advised that if they wanted to avoid consumption, they might want to avoid criminal activity and, thus, stay out of the state prison.

> *The time is fixed, definitely, in the case of about 1,000 of the prisoners. Since the statute restricting convict labor went into effect last July these men have spent all their time in the cells with the exception of forty minutes they are marched around the prison grounds, morning and afternoon, and the time it takes them to eat their meals.*
> *—E.J. Murphy, warden, 1905*

CRUEL TREATMENT AT JOLIET

On May 3, 1905, details of the "cruel and inhuman punishment" meted out to William Cuthbert in the Joliet penitentiary were revealed in court. After seven days in solitary, he was put to work on the stone pile. His hands were swollen, and he couldn't move three fingers on his right hand. A physician testified that Cuthbert was unfit for hard labor. He was "weak, puny, and sickly. (The work) will kill him if he is forced to continue it."

The prisoner had not complained of cruel treatment to any of the prison authorities or to his sister, who visited him. "I said nothing to her about it," he declared, "because I did not wish to cause her further worry. The last time she visited me she broke down and cried, so I kept unpleasant facts from her."

LOCK STEP

In June 1905, the lock step was abolished.

Top: The new dining room meant that men didn't have to eat in their cells anymore. *Courtesy Joliet Area Historical Museum, Illinois.*

Bottom: Marching in lockstep. *Courtesy Joliet Area Historical Museum, Illinois.*

A Daring Attempt at Escape

Vatik Kaminsky attempted to unlock his handcuffs and leap into the Des Plaines River on his way to Joliet Prison. Kaminsky and three others were handcuffed together in pairs. Just before reaching the Des Plaines River bridge, Jailer Whitman, who sat immediately behind the four criminals, noticed their suspicious actions. He leaned over the seat and observed Kaminsky fumbling with his handcuff. A fierce struggle took place in the aisle of the passenger coach, with several passengers trying to help the officer. The convict was finally overpowered and forced down in the seat. A small piece of tin was found in the handcuff—an improvised key that Kaminsky had made himself. It was his intention to leap into the river as the train was crossing the bridge.

Edward Saftig Arrested in St. Louis

Edward Saftig was brought to the Joliet penitentiary from St. Louis to serve out his sentence. The man was an accomplice of Leon Czolgosz, assassin of President William McKinley. He had been paroled the previous June but violated his parole; detectives had been watching for him all over the country. He was apprehended in St. Louis on May 20, 1905. Saftig gained some notoriety shortly after the assassination of McKinley as the one who had tied the handkerchief around the hand of Czolgosz to hide the gun. Czolgosz extended his hand to shake the hand of the president and mortally wounded one of the kindest men of his country.

Convicted Peoria Educator Now "No. 9510"

Newton C. Dougherty began serving his sentence for embezzlement on November 29, 1905. "I must suffer the punishment that my criminal carelessness has brought upon me. I hope to take my punishment like a man," Dougherty said. He did clerical work while he was incarcerated. He was paroled after serving six years for embezzlement but was arrested on new indictments on September 24, 1912.

The men assembled in the chapel for a message. *Courtesy Will County Historical Museum and Research Center.*

Confirmation Services

In December 1905, Archbishop James Edward Quigley of Chicago conducted an impressive confirmation service of the Roman Catholic Church in the penitentiary chapel at Joliet. Kneeling before the altar in the chapel, eight-five prisoners professed to be reclaimed, repeated solemn vows and received the blessing of the archbishop.

A Vicious Attack

In January 1906, a convict by the name of Jones made a murderous attack on the life of Keeper McDonald, who was in charge of the shoe shop of the penitentiary in Joliet. McDonald's scalp was split open four inches by a vicious blow from a hammer.

CONDEMNING THE PRISON

On February 18, 1907, the State Board of Charities made a physical inspection of the prison and reported that the buildings at Joliet were in as good repair as could reasonably be expected. The workshops, storehouses and other utility buildings were spacious, well lit and heated. The refrigerating and heating plants and the plumbing and heating throughout the entire institution were in satisfactory condition.

The men's cell house was the exception. Its ventilation was entirely inadequate. The cells were grouped in the central space of the room, away from windows. No direct sunlight ever entered. Two men shared this small space, using a slop bucket for a toilet. They spent fourteen hours, six days of the week—and on the seventh day nearly twenty-one hours—in this small space. They ate and slept in quarters so contracted and repellant that it was a disgrace.

The women's prison, built twelve years before, was well constructed and well arranged. It was equipped with large cells arranged for one person. Its ventilation permitted a change of air every ten minutes. There was a permanent washbowl and toilet facilities in every cell. Tuberculosis among the female inmates was almost unknown.

Two methods of improving the condition of the convicts were proposed:

> *1. To re-model existing cell houses and build additional cell houses, with modern equipment, including air washing and cleaning devices.*
> *2. To abandon the present site and erect a new prison elsewhere.*

The plan of acquiring a new site and constructing an entirely new prison appeared to be growing in favor. The gradual approach of industrial plants all around the prison, and the increasing menace from smoke and dirt, together with the existing unsanitary conditions in the cell houses, suggested that it would be unwise to spend several thousand dollars rebuilding the cell houses within the present walls. The State Board of Charities recommended that the Joliet penitentiary be removed from its present location to another site about eight miles distant.

LOUIS A. GOURDAIN BUILDS HIS OWN PRISON

In 1907, Louis A. Gourdain was convicted of conducting a lottery. The Chicago banker was sentenced to serve a term of four and a half years in

The cell house. *Courtesy Joliet Area Historical Museum, Illinois.*

the penitentiary for his crime but was released on an appeal through the efforts of his friends—entirely against his wishes. He promised the jury that convicted him that he would serve his sentence, which he regarded as a debt of honor to the government.

Gourdain made several attempts to enter the prison, but Warden Murphy refused to admit him. His plan to build a private jail was the result. "I am going to serve out my sentence in Joliet one way or another," Gourdain said. He went to Washington to implore the U.S. Supreme Court to compel prison authorities to admit him as an inmate for the length of his sentence. Before leaving for Washington, Gourdain packed up his belongings and sent them to Joliet. He negotiated for the lease of a vacant lot opposite the penitentiary grounds. Having formerly been confined at Joliet for twenty-four days as a bookkeeper in the shirt-making department, Gourdain said he knew the place from top to bottom and could build a smaller version.

"I have the whole thing planned out—all I have to do is to let the contract for the work—competitive bids, you know, that's the way the state does in building a penitentiary. I'll have a regular miniature Joliet." He planned to follow all the rules, exactly as inmates of the prison did. He would even hire three guards, one for each eight-hour shift. Louis was successful in getting himself into Joliet but was later transferred to the government prison at Atlanta, Georgia. His family was from New Orleans, so they were able to visit him more frequently there. The transfer was made out of sympathy for his wife.

Louis Gourdain's eccentricities were a favorite of the newspapers. Stories about him ran from coast to coast. Fall River (KS) News, *August 10, 1906.*

ESCAPE FROM THE HOSPITAL

In August 1907, two convicts employed as nurses in the hospital sawed through the iron bars that guarded the second-story window of the hospital, where they slept when off duty. From there, they dropped to the ground and scaled the walls by means of a rope ladder they had made out of bandages taken from the hospital supplies.

THE PRISON CITY

In September 1907, the news reported that Joliet prided itself on being the "Prison City"—but not just because the prison was located there. It had become a center for manufacturers, a well-known supply center for prisons, jails and penal institutions of other cities all over the United States. Constructors of prisons and jails and structural steel were doubling the capacity of their factory because of demand outside of Illinois. The company held contracts for building 230 steel cells in the Indiana State Prison, 200 in the Wisconsin State Prison and 160 in the North Dakota Prison at Bismarck. They had constructed county jails in Virginia, Washington and Mississippi.

Phil Carrol supplied the world with bakers' machinery. The Builders' Supply Company had orders for work in several states, besides its work in Joliet and other Illinois cities. Van Fleet shipped woodwork all over the United States. H.B. Humphrey sent poultry supplies to every state in the union. He also made shipments to Canada, Europe, Honolulu, Russia, Mexico, Australia, South America and Cuba.

BEHIND THE BARS AT THE JOLIET PRISON AND SOME OTHER STUNTS

On November 6, 1907, Sid Wetmore gave a lecture at the Elks Club in Joliet, "Behind the Bars at the Joliet Prison—and Some Other Stunts." He spoke entertainingly to a well-filled room, showing pictures of many noted criminals, views of many departments in the main building and in the women's prison of Joliet. He declared Warden McClaughry one of the foremost criminologists and humanitarians of the day. It was he who had started the ball rolling on prison reform at Joliet. Robert L. Allen and

This collage was likely used in presentations about the penitentiary. *Courtesy Joliet Area Historical Museum, Illinois.*

the present warden, Murphy, had followed in his humane footsteps and instituted further reforms.

JOLIET MURDERERS

Anthony Bluth and Matthew Stariha pled guilty to the murders of August Beltzner and Arthur Yack. The *Streator Free Press* said that they "threw themselves on the mercy of the court rather than run the chances of having a jury hang them, as they hoped that the judge would not sentence them to death." They could be given the death penalty or a sentence beginning at fourteen years. Bluth said that his evil deeds and downfall were due to the influence of Stariha and the reading of dime novels, mentioning the Jesse James and Nick Carter stories, and the witnessing of "cheap sensational plays." The judge ruled that the youths had no regard for human life but were unfit to meet their maker. Thus, both of the teenagers were given life sentences.

HALF HIS LIFE IN PRISON

On December 21, 1908, the story of a young convict was told in the *Joliet Evening Herald-News*. Albert Schupe of Chicago had spent half of his thirty years in prison, nearly seven in the Joliet penitentiary. In his last trial, Schupe was accused of attacking detectives with a revolver.

FORMER CIRCUIT COURT CLERK OF CHICAGO

At the end of January 1908, John A. Cooke, former clerk of the circuit court in Chicago, was brought down and placed in the Joliet penitentiary. He was assigned to the rattan department.

KNOCKS ON DOOR OF THE JOLIET PRISON

Abner Smith, former judge and president of the defunct Bank of North America, knocked at the door of Joliet Prison on June 14, 1909. After his pardon was denied, the former judge went immediately to Joliet accompanied by his brother. When he entered the warden's office, he said that he was there to give himself up. He was told that he could not be admitted without the sheriff's orders. Arrangements were then made for the admission of convict no. 1218.

CRIME ON THE RISE

An article in the *Joliet Evening Herald-News* of January 2, 1910, said that Joliet's rapid stride toward metropolitan heights had found a barometric recorder in its police department records. A varied assortment of crimes from murder to manslaughter to common disorderly conduct and intoxication could be found in the 1909 calendar. The closing year had shown an abandonment of "small-town" criminal events and wove many an interesting chapter.

Fresh flowers were put together for the warden's quarters. *Courtesy Will County Historical Museum and Research Center.*

THE PRISON GETS POWER

On February 10, 1910, the Illinois Penitentiary Commissioners entered into a contract with the sanitary district for electrical power for operating the manufacturing plants and lighting the prison. The meeting reviewed bids for the contract from the Economy Light and Power Company and the Joliet Sanitary District. The agreement had a life of three years with the right of renewal at the end of that period. Other action taken by the commissioners called for an appropriation by the state legislature of $25,000 for the erection of the destroyed powerhouse and a reward of $250 to the Joliet Fire Department for services rendered at a fire the week before.

SAMUEL MOSER

On March 14, 1910, Samuel Moser committed suicide at the state prison by hanging himself with a rope made from his bed clothing. His body was found hanging from the window by one of the guards. The *Woodford County Journal* reported that Moser had been in feeble health for several months. He was known to be subject to melancholy periods. While he was in the midst of one of these, on May 13, 1900, Samuel murdered his wife and three children. He was sentenced to twenty-one years in the penitentiary at Joliet. (Sam's story is told in the book *So Many Fragile Things* by Amy Steidinger (2020).)

A Stolen Buggy

Frank Fuller was sent to Joliet for theft. He maintained his innocence so earnestly that he was paroled in April 1910. He was given a position with the Powers and Williams hardware company. He worked steadily and gained the confidence of the boss and employees who worked with him. He was given a key to the warehouse, wherein was kept the larger tools and vehicles. One night, he appeared at a saloon and offered to sell a wagon to some horse traders. After the deal was made, it was suggested that Fuller might have stolen the buggy. They demanded that the money be returned and that Fuller take back the vehicle. Fuller then offered to give the road wagon to the traders for nothing. The bar owner went to the home of Officer Hopkins and told him the story. The policeman found out that the buggy had been taken from the Powers and Williams warehouse. His boss said that Williams had not shown up for work. The suspect was located and placed under arrest. When questioned, he said that he was making the deal for Mr. Williams. Confronted with the facts, Fuller finally admitted the crime and was returned to prison.

Crescent City Murders

In May 1910, Lucy B. Sayler and Dr. William Miller, convicted murderers of John Sayler, the Crescent City banker, were brought to Joliet and placed in the penitentiary to serve the three- and twelve-year sentences imposed on them respectively by a jury sitting in Watseka five weeks before.

James Ryan

On May 20, 1910, the lifeless form of James Ryan was found dangling by a prison guard from a rafter in the chair shop. The thirty-year-old was serving his second term at the Illinois State Penitentiary for burglary. During the noon hour, Ryan went to the shop, made a piece of rope into a noose, climbed a rafter and jumped into eternity. Ryan was known as a runner in the prison. He had the freedom of the yard and acted as a messenger between the various shops. Little attention was paid to his absence, as he was often on these missions. Just before the men returned to work, one of the guards went into the chair shop. He happened to glance up and see Ryan. He summoned assistance, and the body was cut down. The prison physician was called, but Ryan's life had ended when he reached the scene.

A Fire in the Shirt Factory

In July 1910, crossed electric wires were determined to have been the cause of a $20,000 fire at the State Prison in Joliet. The fire broke out in the shirt factory and was stubborn in extreme, the heavy slate roof confining its zone and filling the interior with dense smoke that practically defied the efforts of the firefighters to penetrate it. The building was repaired at once.

Foreign Dignitaries

On September 24, 1910, a delegation of fifty men and women visited the state prison in Joliet. The delegates to the International Prison Congress were leaders in educational and political circles from countries from all over the world. After the meeting of the congress in Washington, D.C., they traveled in a special train and stopped at larger cities, where penal institutions were visited. Some things noted by the visitors included: contents of the beef stew and the speed with which the prisoners devoured it; descriptions of pictures and names of books found in the prisoners' cells; degrees of happiness and discontent noted among the convicts; and conclusions on the fact that half of the female inmates were African American women.

Making Better Men

December 14, 1910—There are few people these days who stop to think about the man who is in prison. Even fewer visit and give him a word of encouragement. In the old days, George Vance and others went to the prison on Sunday afternoons and told the prisoners about the wonderful love God had for them. That story made better men. When he came out into the world again, the ex-convict had love in his heart and not a feeling of revenge against society in general. Strange, is it not, that we do not exhibit it more often to those who need it most?

William Robinson

On December 28, 1910, William Robinson, sixty-six years of age, stood before the judge and asked that he be sent back to Joliet. His wish was granted, because he was arrested for a serious offense. Robinson had already spent thirty-two years in various prisons. "Joliet prison is the best that I ever was in," he said. "I suppose I will die in prison. All that I ask is that they give me an even number. I don't like odd numbers."

Behind the Bars at Joliet

On February 10, 1911 the Star Theater secured a big feature attraction, the sensational illustrated lecture "Behind the Bars at Joliet." Paul G. Baxter was employed at the prison for ten years. His pictures were the only ones in existence showing the interior and exterior of the Joliet penitentiary and women's prison. He told how 1,600 of the most desperate criminals in the world were kept in confinement, subjection and at work.

Chicken Farm

It was announced on March 29, 1911, that the state penitentiary was going into the chicken industry. Peter Van Vlissingen, the confessed forger of $700,000, was made caretaker of two incubators that had just been installed. By the next fall, Warden Murphy expected to have one thousand chickens on his hands. A brooder house with a capacity of three thousand was being built. The incubators were placed near Van Vlissingen's room. "I expect to be out of this prison in about a year, and I intend to go into the chicken business. This will be excellent education for me," he said.

A convict in stripes tends the lawn near the guardhouse. *Courtesy Joliet Area Historical Museum, Illinois.*

SUSPICIOUS QUESTIONS

On the afternoon of Saturday, May 20, 1911, six convicts escaped from the penitentiary under the darkness caused by a sudden storm. About 240 men were at work in the prison quarry, a block away from the prison. They marched to and from the prison under guard. A storm came up suddenly about 4:00 p.m. Before the men could be started back to the prison, it became dark as night. Later, the count showed six men missing. One was recaptured two hours later in McCoy's Woods. Joseph Pryor recognized the prison stripes and overcame the man after a fight. Another was taken back by two railroad detectives who spotted him just as he was about to enter the deep woods. The other four were gone.

On May 29, a fellow appeared in Freeport, asking for something to eat. He was dirty and wore a big slouch hat, which he refused to take off. He asked if the men who had escaped from Joliet Prison had been captured. He wanted to see newspapers and looked over them hurriedly. The man ate five sandwiches, six doughnuts and meat and drank three cups of coffee. He asked if he could leave through a back fence, stating that there was a large dog up the street. The hosts did not report the man until it was too late but said that he left in the direction of the railroad yards.

The Union Depot

Preferring death to a prison term, Lillian McDowell attempted suicide in June 1911 by jumping from an Alton train at the Union Depot in Chicago. The woman was being taken to the Joliet penitentiary to serve time for stealing diamonds valued at $1,000.

Haldane Cleminson

On May 30, 1909, Nora Jane Cleminson was found dead in her apartments. Her husband said that he had been chloroformed along with his wife by burglars. The coroner found no trace of chloroform poisoning but said that morphine had killed her. Later, a woman named Anna Schmidt came forward with the story that she had been with Dr. Cleminson the night of the supposed crime. Cleminson had tried to make it appear that he had been chloroformed by the burglars in order that his acts on the night of his wife's death would not be scrutinized. A rehearing in light of this new evidence was denied, and Dr. Haldane Cleminson was brought to the penitentiary in Joliet in June 1911. He was sentenced to life behind bars for murdering his wife. Cleminson was instrumental in analyzing evidence in the murder investigation of Odette Allen after her murder in the prison. He was pardoned in July 1919.

Dr. Harry Elgin Webster

On September 10, 1911, Dr. Harry Elgin Webster, a young Chicago physician, stabbed his bigamous second wife, Bessie Kent Webster, to death in a ravine near Dixon, Illinois. He first said that he would never plead guilty but later declared that he had no regrets and was willing to pay the penalty.

In August 1914, attorney James E. Callahan wrote to the English surgeon general:

We are applying for the pardon of Drs. Haldane Cleminson and Harry E. Webster, two young surgeons who are under life sentences for murder. Both are expert young surgeons and have made excellent records as prisoners. They have been in prison for about three years. In conversation with them recently they expressed a desire to join the surgical staff of one of the armies now engaged in war with Europe. If pardoned, and we are directing this letter to you to inquire whether or not, if the governor of Illinois should grant them pardons, you can give them work on the field of battle. We beg to advise you that we believe Dr. Cleminson entirely innocent of the charge of murder that was placed against him. Dr. Webster confessed to having killed his wife. We do not hesitate to say that these men would be a credit to your surgical staff and to the British flag. They are only humans who may or may not have erred. They are not only willing but also anxious to risk their lives if they can by their skill, relieve the sufferings of their fellowmen on the battlefield.

GRACE FULLER

Grace Fuller began her career as a schoolteacher. She was for nine years dean of women at the Michigan State Normal School at Ypsilanti, Michigan. She was matron of the women's state prison at Joliet from 1912 to 1922. She taught the inmates domestic science, cooking, sewing and general housework. She retired in 1922. She died at the Illinois Soldiers' Widows' Home in 1968 at the age of ninety-six.

GEORGE CRUMLEY

On March 19, 1912, George Crumley, who was committed to Joliet Prison in the circuit court of Woodford County about five years before, died of consumption. He had been sick and failing for a year, and although he worked in the open air, the disease progressed until he was finally summoned from this life. He was thirty-six years of age and had been at Joliet for five years and one month. He was buried there.

Croquet on the lawn. *Courtesy Joliet Area Historical Museum, Illinois.*

A Trio of Trusties Escapes

On Sunday, October 27, 1912, a trio of convicts escaped from Joliet. The trusties had been sent to the boiler house to repair a broken pipe around midnight. They instead climbed over the north wall with the aid of an improvised ladder. On Monday night, the trio appeared before a towerman for the Michigan Central at Chicago Heights and demanded that the railroad employee shed his clothing. All three were in prison garb. Just as the man was stripping off his vest, the telephone bell rang in the tower, and the convicts fled.

The next day, a farmer saw a man wearing a prison uniform. He notified the police, who were on the alert for the fugitive. He was captured and identified as Tony Saunders. He was armed with a loaded .44-caliber revolver but gave himself up without a struggle, declaring that he was thinking of his mother and would rather submit peaceably than have more crimes attached to his record. He warned police that the others were armed and would put up a fight. They were in a field nearby. The police, armed with Winchester repeating rifles, surrounded the field. A large force of prison guards arrived shortly after the police, and a chain of officers was woven about the territory. The two convicts were arrested without incident. After a customary period in the solitary unit, they would be dressed in red suits and would have to carry a ball and chain.

TYPHOID FEVER

On October 29, 1912, it was reported that Joliet was facing a typhoid epidemic. In the first ward, serious cases were increasing daily.

POLITICIANS ASK PARDONS BEFORE DENEEN RETIRES

Governor Deneen considered pardons for prisoners before he retired from office. On November 19, 1912, a pardon was asked for George Gill Roberts, serving a thirty-year sentence for the murder of Cook County commissioner John V. Kopf. The widow was there with the lawyers opposing the action and wept as the facts were retold. C.W. Church sought a pardon for Roy Powell, serving a long term for the murder of Professor J. Workinger, a hypnotist. When the crime was committed in 1901, Powell was nineteen years old. He had quarreled with the man, picked up a heavy piece of iron and struck him, instantly killing him.

Senator Brady petitioned for the pardon of William Roach, who had served nineteen years for the murder of a Chicago policeman. Roach had been a model convict. Senator Clark asked for the pardon of L. White, who had killed a man during a game of craps. White was only eighteen years old at the time, and it was claimed that he had acted in self-defense. He bore marks said to have been inflicted by the victim during the fight.

CONVICTS MARVEL AT SKYSCRAPERS

On December 1, 1912, Thomas McNally and Charles Kurth were taken to Chicago to testify in court in the hope of securing their freedom from prison. Both men were veterans of the Civil War and had not been outside the prison in eighteen years. They marveled at the world's progress, having never seen a trolley car or an automobile. They were serving sentences for the murder of James Prunty and his son and the shooting of a daughter. They had maintained their innocence from the time of their arrest. An

Convicts were amazed at the skyscrapers after years behind bars. This is a view of Randolph and Dearborn looking south in 1909. *Chicago Historical Society*.

effort was being made to secure their release. Prominent war veterans of Chicago were behind the men.

Life Termers Take on the Legislature

The next day, on December 2, 1912, an organization was formed among the "life termers," who asked that a law be enacted in Illinois making it possible for convicts serving life sentences to be paroled. The movement was backed by over one hundred prisoners serving sentences at Joliet Prison. Many of the "lifers" believed themselves to be much better men and entitled to more consideration than prisoners who had served several terms and who had broken their paroles at various times.

The idea met the approval of Warden E.J. Murphy, who said: "I would rather have 100 life men around me than a dozen of burglars, pickpocket thieves, highwaymen and the like. A large percentage of the murders they are charged with were committed on the spur of the moment and their past records show absolutely no criminal traces."

Warren Sanders

Warren Sanders entered the prison gates on February 4, 1913, to serve a life sentence for the murder of his wife and mother-in-law. The young man said he had no malice in his heart and hoped to make a good record. He earnestly said that no officers needed to accompany him, that he was willing and ready to take the trip to Joliet alone. His offer was not accepted by the sheriff. He asked friends to keep an eye on his daughter and to write to him as often as possible concerning her. He hoped to be released from prison and to be able to devote himself to the care of his child. In July 1926, Sanders severed the arteries in both wrists by battering away the glass on his cell door. Prison officials said he would recover.

Corsets in Prison

In March 1913, Minona S. Jones was quoted as saying that "when a woman loses her waistline, her self-respect goes also. Forbidden the corset, she takes a step downward in the moral scale. She can't be good." The treatment of women in Illinois State institutions was denounced. "The women in Joliet prison are treated worse than cattle. Give them pretty clothes and surroundings of a reformatory instead of a penal institution and they will make better wives for average men than the girls to be met in society." Another lecture was delivered by Mrs. John J. Hessler, who declared that women attired in the extremes of modern fashion are unconscious contributors to the growth of vice.

The Years of Reform

On April 26, 1913, Warden Edmund M. Allen took over as warden of Joliet Prison. His policies for humanizing prison administration attracted widespread attention. He ordered that convicts be permitted to converse with one another, an unheard-of thing. "It is the silent man who conspires," he explained. "Force a man into moodiness by refusing to permit him to talk to his fellows and he will occupy his mind plotting. Give him a chance to air his views among his fellow prisoners" and he will feel contented when he gets through. He defended their right to complain, saying, "kicking is a great American privilege and a convict feels like a human being when he has a chance to indulge in it to his heart's content."

A guard watches a line of prisoners march by, cane at the ready. *Courtesy Will County Historical Museum and Research Center.*

Allen knew all about prison life. His father was warden of the prison when he was a boy. There were "lifers" in Joliet who recalled the youngster in knickerbockers. Some of the trusties still called him "Eddie." The banishment of the "silence rule" was only one of several changes Allen made in his uplift policy at Joliet.

Prison stripes were abolished and solid prison gray-blue substituted. Only escaped convicts who had returned and those who violated their paroles were distinguished by clothing from the others. They alone still wore the crossbar suits of black and white.

In 2018, the Joliet Area Historical Museum began running tours of the penitentiary for Route 66 travelers. It offers a one-and-a-half-hour walking tour that covers the general history of the prison from 1858 to the present. The Haunted History Tour covers the darker stories of the historic prison as you walk through the prison at dusk. The Guard Tour is led by two docents who worked at the prison while it was still in operation until 2002. They tell of daily life at the prison during their time there—a more personal take on the site's history. The Photography Tour is a four-hour tour of the expansive prison site. People take photos in the morning light with supervised access to the prison yard and predesignated buildings. Tickets can be purchased online at Jolietprison.org.

BIBLIOGRAPHY

Adam, David. "Does a New Genetic Analysis Finally Reveal the Identity of Jack the Ripper?" Sciencemag.org, March 15, 2019. https://www.sciencemag.org.

Bell, Don. "McGill Grad Took His Secret to the Gallows." *The Gazette* (Montreal, Quebec, Canada), February 26, 1979.

Dodge, L. Mara. *Whores and Thieves of the Worst Kind: A Study of Women, Crime, and Prisons, 1885–2000*. DeKalb: Northern Illinois University Press, 2006.

Green, James. *Death in the Haymarket*. New York: Anchor Books, 2006.

McLaren, Angus. *A Prescription for Murder: The Victorian Serial Killings of Dr. Thomas Neill Cream*. Chicago: University of Chicago Press, 1995.

McMichael, T.H. "Robert Wilson McClaughry: 1839–1920." *Journal of the Illinois State Historical Society* 13, no. 4 (January 1921): 598–610.

Perrot, Mollie. "A Body Found: The Case of Charlie Ford and the Conspirators." *The Times* (Streator, IL), November 30, 2009.

———. "Execution of Charles Ford." *The Times*, December 7, 2009.

Taylor, Henry J. "How 'Grave' Mistake Sealed Fate of Lincoln Body Snatchers." *Pittsburgh (PA) Press*, March 3, 1973.

INDEX

ABOUT THE AUTHOR

Amy has spent the last twenty-five years as a teacher and a genealogist. Many of her years teaching were spent working in juvenile justice. She went back to school and earned a master's degree in history from Illinois State University. She loves to travel and is always planning the next adventure. Her greatest joy is her family—her husband, Jay, and their four children, who have grown up to be amazing adults.